NORTH EAST GERMAN
GERMAN
NARROW GAUGE
Harz Mountains and Baltic Region

John Organ

MP Middleton Press

Front Cover: Two of the LKM built metre gauge 2-10-2Ts meet at Drei Annen Hohne on the Harz system. No. 99 7233-2 arrives with a train from Nordhausen whilst no. 99 7238-1 was in the course of being prepared for the long ascent to the Brocken Summit on 16th October 1995. (J.F.Organ).
Rear Cover: One of the "Molli" Orenstein & Koppel 2-8-2Ts, no. 99 2322-8, has just replenished its water tanks and coal bunker at Kühlungsborn West prior to hauling a train to Bad Doberan on 12th May 2004. (J.F.Organ).

Published.November 2004

ISBN 1 904474 44 6

© *Middleton Press, 2004*

Design   Deborah Esher
*   David Pede*

Published by
*   Middleton Press*
*   Easebourne Lane*
*   Midhurst, West Sussex*
*   GU29 9AZ*
Tel: 01730 813169
Fax: 01730 812601
Email: info@middletonpress.co.uk
www.middletonpress.co.uk

Printed & bound by MPG Books, Bodmin.. Cornwall

CONTENTS

ACKNOWLEDGEMENTS

In compiling this publication, I have been very fortunate in having received much valuable assistance from a large number of fellow enthusiasts. My thanks are due to Mr. J. Bell, Mr and Mrs B. Benn, Mr. J. Dobson, Mr. A. Heywood, Mr. J. Marsh, Mr. T. Martin, Mr. D. Trevor Rowe, Mr. S. Sedgwick, Mr. J. Snell and Mr. K.Taylorson. The series editor has provided the words to his own photographs.

A special word of thanks is especially due to John Bell, my contact in Germany, without whose invaluable assistance the Harz section would be far from complete. John has specifically asked me to record the fact that much of his information was gleaned from German publications, some of which are now out of print. Therefore due acknowledgement must be made to the following authors, Jörg Bauer, Hans Röper, Thomas Knop, Friedrich Metge and Gerhard Zieglgansberger. Likewise, publications by Lothar Schultz and Detlef Radke have been an invaluable source of reference for the Baltic and Brandenburg section.

Finally I must add a special word of thanks to my wife Brenda, who has once again tolerated my deep involvement in the subject during the period of research and compilation.

I.   Location map in 1964.

1. HARZER SCHMALSPUR BAHNEN
2. EISFELD - SCHÖNBRUNN
3. GERA - MEUSELWITZ
4. BAD DOBERAN - KÜHLUNGSBORN
5. RÜGEN
6. FRANZBURGER KREISBAHNEN
7. MECKLENBURG - POMMERSCHE
8. PRIGNITZER KREISKLEINBAHNEN
9. KLEINBAHN KREIS JERICHOW
10. JÜTERBOG - LUCKENWAKDER KREISKLEINBAHNEN

INTRODUCTION

During the last decade of the 19th Century and the first half of the 20th Century, Germany boasted a colossal network of narrow gauge railways. These extensive systems were to be found throughout this large country, although the greatest proliferation was to be found in the east. Following World War 2 and the division of Germany by the Iron Curtain, the large systems in the Saxony, Harz and Baltic regions were all transferred to the newly formed German Democratic Republic (GDR) and controlled by the state system Deutsche Reichsbahn (DR) until the reunification of Germany in 1990. Between 1920 and 1945 many of the lines, notably those in Saxony, had been under the control of the predecessor of DR, Deutsche Reichsbahn-Gesellschaft (DRG).

The majority of lines that remained in West Germany were closed during the 1950s and 1960s, as part of modernisation and co-ordination schemes. However, many of those in East Germany were saved as a result of the severe austerity implemented by the communist government and lack of investment to modernise the rail network. Consequently when the two countries were reunited and the former DR systems were transferred either to Deutsche Bahn (DB) or newly formed private consortiums, there existed a veritable "time warp" of narrow gauge railways still relying on steam haulage and providing an everyday service of both passenger and freight trains. Needless to say the decade since reunification has by necessity seen many changes, although steam still reigns supreme on the surviving lines. The locomotives are mainly powerful 2-10-2Ts, many of which were built during the 1950s, together with articulated machines in the form of 0-4-4-0T Meyers and Mallets of an earlier vintage.

In a publication of this size it would be impossible to cover all the narrow gauge railways in a large country the size of Germany. Consequently it will concentrate upon a selection of the systems that were formerly behind the Iron Curtain in the GDR of which many have survived to become a mecca for steam enthusiasts world-wide. The systems covered include the large metre gauge network in the Harz Mountains, the varied 75cm and 60cm lines in Brandenburg and the Baltic region, plus the unique 90cm line in the latter area. The numerous 75cm systems in Saxony will be covered in a separate volume, together with 60cm and 38cm (15 inch) miniature lines in that area.

Due to its close proximity to the Iron Curtain, photography of the Harz system was a practice frowned upon by the authorities. Consequently the photographic coverage in this publication devoted to that large network of lines is mainly from the post reunification period. The views that were captured during the GDR era, especially those at Wernigerode, were no doubt taken after a quick look over the shoulder to ensure that no prying eyes were in evidence! However, the railways further away from the border in Brandenburg and the Baltic regions were considerably more approachable. We are fortunate that some enthusiasts were able to visit and photograph the activities of these systems during the period of the "cold war", with the result that some unrepeatable scenes have been recorded for posterity.

Despite the austere conditions that the citizens of the GDR were forced to endure, it is gratifying to record that the East German Government appreciated the historic nature of the surviving narrow gauge railways within their country. In 1975, all the remaining lines in the areas covered by this publication were accorded the status of National Technical Monuments, a fact that has undoubtedly assisted their continued survival into the 21st century. Even so, some of these lines were threatened with closure around the time of reunification. Fortunately this action proved unnecessary due to the political upheaval, which allowed time for a complete review of the situation.

An example of practices from the past was the use of a departure board consisting of small enamelled metal tablets. This was recorded at Alexisbad in 1996. (V. Mitchell).

PART ONE
METRE GAUGE LINES IN THE HARZ MOUNTAINS

The Harz Mountain range lies roughly in the centre of Germany. Formed of both granite and limestone they are also rich in deposits of copper, lead, silver and zinc. Additionally, the lower slopes are dense forestry plantations, which have maintained a rich harvest of timber. Although not the most lofty mountains in Germany, the highest peak being the 1142m (3769 ft) Brocken, it is certainly an area of outstanding scenic attraction in many ways reminiscent of Snowdonia. During the period of the Cold War and the division of Germany, the Iron Curtain ran through the centre of the mountain range whilst the Soviet authorities established a very sensitive "listening post" on the summit of the Brocken.

Plans to construct a railway network in the Harz region in order to tap the valuable mineral deposits were first mooted in 1866. However, following many failed proposals it was to be a further 20 years before any definite progress was made. In its final development, the 132km metre gauge Harz network was comprised of two separate companies, which together formed roughly a "Y" shaped system with a main line connection at each extremity of the three arms. The two companies concerned were the Gernrode HarzgeroderEisenbahn (GHE) which

was completed in 1886 and the Nordhausen Wernigerode Eisenbahn (NWE) which began operations in 1897. The two independent concerns where eventually joined by a short connecting line built by the GHE in 1905. The three main line connections were at Wernigerode and Gernrode on the two northern ends of the "Y" and Nordhausen to the south.

In addition to the two systems mentioned above, there was a third metre gauge line in the Harz area. This was the 24km Südharzeisenbahn (South Harz Railway) which opened in 1899 linking Walkenried and Braunlage, with an 8km branch from Brunnenbachsmühle to Tanne. Following the division of Germany after World War 2, this line was dissected by the Iron Curtain. The majority lay in West Germany and was closed in 1963 whilst the short stretch in the GDR, on the branch to Tanne, operated a limited freight only service until 1958. This line had originally crossed the NWE at Sorge, which was situated close to the border and not surprisingly was cut off from the remainder of the route following the creation of the new state. The main line of the system was noted for its steep gradients and curvaceous route as it climbed northwards from Walkenried on the western flank of the Harz Mountains.

1. Gernrode Harzgerode Eisenbahn

Although not as strategically important as the NWE, the GHE was nevertheless the first part of the Harz system to be completed. The first section though the delightful Selke Valley linking Gernrode and Hasselfelde, with a short steep branch to Harzgerode, was opened in stages between 1887 and 1892 with a total distance of 43km. The main reason for its construction was to connect Harzgerode and the many small villages along the route with the main line network at Gernrode. Following the construction of the NWE a decade later, the 9km extension from Stiege to Eisfelder Talmühle was completed in 1905 in order to connect the two systems. Although there was a connecting line between the GHE and NWE at Eisfelder Talmühle, the

two railways had separate tracks and platforms at this joint station.

During the first half century of its existence the GHE led a fairly uneventful existence, somewhat overshadowed by its larger and more important neighbouring line. However, following the turmoil and aftermath of World War 2 the original section of the line between Gernrode and Stiege (apart for approximately 1km west of Strassberg) together with the Harzgerode branch, was dismantled and transported to Russia in 1946 as reparations. Rolling stock and all but one of the locomotives were also dispatched along with the track and sleepers. The one surviving locomotive was left behind to work a connecting line to a mine from Strassberg (Lindenberg until

1952). Meanwhile a diminutive railcar was saved simply because at the time it was stored in a shed belonging to the NWE at Eisfelder Talmühle, the latter concern having taken over the operation of the line to Stiege and Hasselfelde which served some important stone quarries near Eisfelder. In April 1949 the NWE and re-emerging GHE were absorbed by Deutsche Reichsbahn (DR), the communist regime stating that all private companies were to be state owned.

The GDR realised within a very short time that the economic survival of the Selke Valley was dependent upon the reinstatement of the railway that had been so savagely torn up and removed to Russia. Even before the incorporation in DR, relaying of the track began at the end of 1946 under the auspices of the local council, the railwaymen and the Sächsischen Provinzialbahnen GmbH. By March 1949 the route through the valley from Gernrode to Alexisbad and Strassberg was re-opened for freight traffic with full services recommencing in May of that year. The branch from Alexisbad to Harzgerode was reinstated in July 1950. The surviving locomotive, a 0-6-0T now renumbered as DR no. 99.5811, was augmented by other equipment transferred from the former NWE. Thus the railway was very soon able to serve the numerous industrial connections between Alexisbad and Strassberg again. The freight traffic was so heavy in the early 1950s that trains continued to run throughout the night, the main traffic being fluorspar, timber, metal goods and explosives. In 1966, however, a centralised transport plan decreed that the line should be closed from the early 1970s and the traffic transferred to the state road hauliers. From that time, only emergency repairs were carried out on the infrastructure and stock. Fortunately in September 1972 the transport ministry did an "about turn" and put the line, together with the Harzquer and Brocken lines, under a preservation order as a technical monument. In 1973 the DR even planned to rebuild the missing section between Strassberg and Stiege, thereby reconnecting the two isolated sections of metre gauge railway. Due to economic restraints it was to be 1982 before the work actually began. The connecting link was re-opened in 1984 and led to a further development in the opening out of the loading gauge between Gernrode and Harzgerode to allow the freight to be handled in standard gauge wagons on transporters. This signalled the end of the use of narrow gauge freight wagons on the system.

As a result of a coal-fired power station being built at Silberhütte, heavy coal trains from Nordhausen with standard gauge wagons carried on transporter vehicles were to become a common feature at this time. These were often double-headed on the steep gradients between Ilfeld and Stiege. As reversal was necessary at Stiege, a turning circle was constructed in order to speed up this operation and to minimise the manhandling of the heavy coupling bars to the transporter wagons. Although the coal trains are now a distant memory, following the closure and demolition of the power station in 1992, the turning circle still survives and is often used by special trains when the need arises.

Following German reunification, the former GHE and NWE lines were transferred from DR control on February 1st 1993 to a newly formed private company the Harzer Schmalspurbahn GmbH (HSB) with 20,000,000 DM starting capital being provided by DR. The shareholders in this company are the district councils of Wernigerode, Nordhausen and Quedlinburg together with other communities on the routes. Substantial financial backing continues from the states of Saxon-Anhalt and Thüringen.The new administration, although operating the whole network as a single railway, has split the system into three sections for marketing purposes. The old GHE section between Gernrode and Eisfelder Talmühle is now known as Die Selketalbahn (Selke Valley Railway) and is comprised of a delightful rural railway, 52km in length. Throughout the 1990s much of the track has been upgraded and many of the open level crossings fitted with half barriers to improve safety. From the mid-1990s many of the services have been operated by railcars. Steam still reaches Harzgerode and Hasselfelde every day, with extra steam hauled services at weekends between April and October.

The journey along the Selketalbahn begins at Gernrode, where the metre gauge station and three road locomotive depot is situated alongside the now closed standard gauge station, which was on a branch of the route from Hannover to Leipzig. The metre gauge line curves away in a southerly direction and passes through an area of dense forest soon climbing at 1 in 30 to reach the first summit at Sternhaus Ramberg, 7km from Gernrode. From here the line descends at 1 in 25, the steepest section on the whole system, to reach the Selke valley at Mägdesprung (10km). The line continues, now gently uphill again to reach the junction station at Alexisbad (15km). Here the 3km steeply graded branch leaves the main line and begins to climb in an easterly direction on a ruling gradient of 1 in 30 as it curves around amid rugged cliff faces towards the terminus at the historic town of Harzgerode. Until recently Alexisbad was renowned for its parallel departures as trains bound for Harzgerode and Hasselfelde departed simultaneously, the locomotive hauling the train on the branch line attempting to stay alongside the main line train locomotive despite the adverse gradient that begins immediately after the station. In recent years, with many of the services on this section of the HSB being handled by railcars, this dramatic practice has ceased although it is recreated on special occasions.

The continuing journey, along the main line towards Stiege, passes through the valley floor on a gentle uphill grade alongside meadows and streams that merge into ponds and rushing torrents. A string of picturesque villages and hamlets are passed, each with its small station or halt, until the junction at Stiege, 36 km from Gernrode, is approached from the south. Here is situated the aforementioned turning circle

to the north of the station, alongside the line to Hasselfelde (40km). Before reaching Stiege the character of the line changes dramatically. The route now passes over a bare windswept landscape reminiscent of that found in parts of Northern France, whilst the Brocken mountain can be clearly seen in the distance to the north-west. The line ends abruptly at the station at Hasselfelde, with only a small shelter and a recently opened restaurant in the former station building for passenger amenities, which lies on the edge of the town. A connecting line to a former timber yard continued on from the head-shunt and the old goods warehouse stands next to the single road engine shed, which was in use until the early 1990s. The shed now houses one of the "mothballed" 2-10-2s, no.99 7244-9, which is occasionally pulled outside as a visitor attraction.

Finally, the 9km line from Stiege to Eisfelder Talmühle continues first uphill over moorland to a halt at Birkenmoor. There then follows a steep descent at 1 in 27 through more woodland, passing a large stone quarry that was the main reason for this section of the old GHE being retained in 1945. One of the principal products of the quarry is ballast of which there is a regular transport in standard gauge wagons to the main line system at Nordhausen. The Selketalbahn route enters the major junction station at Eisfelder from the north, passing alongside the line from Wernigerode for the final few metres. The three-road station is situated within a deep wooded valley dominated by a large half-timber framed station building, this style of architecture being typical of the area.

July 1913

GERNRODE and EISFELDER.

Gernrode ...dep	7a25	9a20	1155	1p25	2p25	4p15	...	6p47	7p55	**Eisfelder** dep	...	6a51	...	10a15	...	...	3 p0	4p45	7p25
Alexisbad.........arr	8 9	10 7	1239	2 15	3 10	4 59	...	7 34	8 44	Stiege........arr	...	7 13	...	10 37	...	...	3 26	5 11	7 47
Harzgerode ...arr	8 25	1021	1254	...	3 26	5 13	...	7 49	9 2	Hasselfelde dp	...	...	...	10 15	...	...	3 7	...	7 25
Alexisbad........dep	8 14	1013		2 25		5 0	...		8 50	Stiege ......dep	...	7 16	...	10 42	...	...	3 32	5 16	7 51
Stiege............arr	9 5	11 8	...	3 32	...	6 9	7p55	..	9 50	Alexisbad...arr	...	8 8	...	11 47	...	pm	4 36	6 25	8 42
Hasselfelde ...arr	9 32	1132	...	3 49	...	6 15		8 12	...	1017	Harzgerodedp	...	7 53	9a50	10 35	1 p5	258	4 42	6 46	8 25
Stiege,...............dep	9 8	1112	...	3 57	...	6 15			...	9 54	Alexisbad dep	6a14	8 13	10 0	12 8	1 16	313	4 59	7 2	8 47
Eisfelder 165B arr	9 30	1134	...	4 6	...	6 43	...		...	1022	**Gernrode** arr	7 0	9 0	1137	1 1	4 2	5 4 3	5 50	7 54	9 36

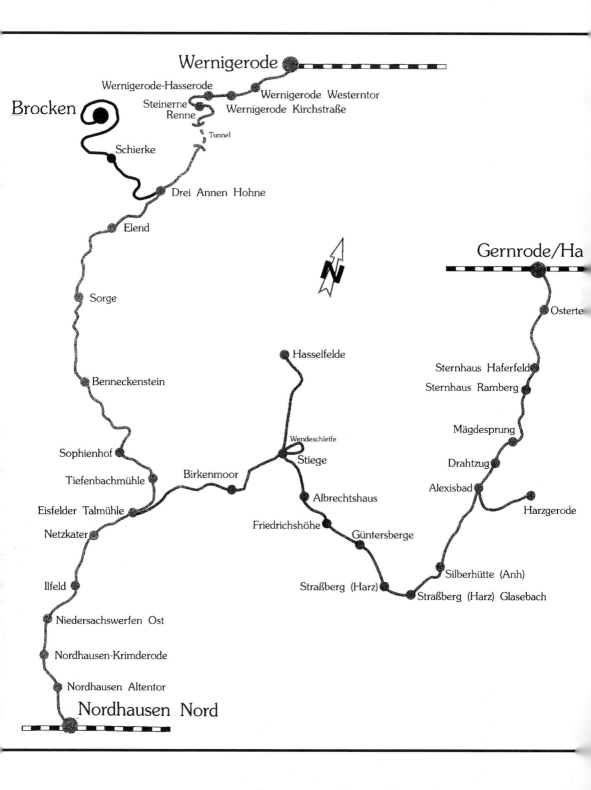

1.1.   A scene at Gernrode on 14th April 1976 as Jung 0-4-4-0T Mallet no. 99 5904 arrives with a train from Alexisbad. At that time when reunification was a long way in the future, this section of the Harz system was isolated from the remainder of the network and worked as a separate self-contained railway. (K.Taylorson).

1.2.   Two decades later at the same location, the two sections of the Harz network have been reconnected and the system privatised. M.G.Karlsruhe 0-4-4-0T Mallet no. 99 5906-5 prepares to depart from Gernrode with a train bound for Harzgerode in June 1996. (R.White -J.F.Organ. coll.)

1.3.　A closer record of the 1949 station earlier in 1996 includes the locomotive shed on the left. In the distance is the goods depot. This had been the terminal building until 1946. (V. Mitchell).

1.4.　The smoke on the left of the previous picture was coming from Mallet no. 99 5906-5 which has now moved away from the shed. The scene is from 24th February 1996, when the snow plough had recently returned from active service. (V. Mitchell).

1.5.   The Krupp 2-6-2T no. 99 6001-4 crosses the completely unprotected level crossing at Gernrode as it departs with a train bound for Alexisbad and Hasselfelde on 22nd May 2004. (J.F.Organ).

1.6.   Alexisbad station with no. 99 6001-4 taking water whilst Mallet no. 99 5906-5 is about to depart with a train bound for Harzgerode on 22nd May 2004. (J.F.Organ).

1.7.   The diminutive railcar no. 187 001, formerly GHE no. T1, pauses at Alexisbad with a special charter from Gernrode on 19th October 1995. (J.F.Organ).

1.8.   Until quite recently, parallel departures from Alexisbad where a daily occurrence. With many services on this section now handled by railcars plus a less intensive timetable, scenes like this with a pair of 2-10-2Ts storming away from the station together are reserved for special occasions. No. 99 7232-4 is bound for Eisfelder Talmühle whilst no. 99 7240-7 attacks the incline to Harzgerode on 15th August 1992. (Mrs B. Benn).

1.9.   During the short period it was running with its NWE number of 21 and green livery restored, the Krupp 2-6-2T storms up the 1 in 30 gradient from Alexisbad to Harzgerode on 7th May 1992. (B. Benn).

1.10. Three views of the branch terminus at Harzgerode date from 24th February 1996. This is from the top of the incline and includes the 16.57 departure, together with the run-round loop. (V. Mitchell).

1.11. The rear of the two-coach train is alongside the goods shed. This was probably then a world record for the shortest entirely regularly steam-worked branch. (V. Mitchell).

1.12. The Mallet has been seen already at Gernrode (picture 1.4), where it started its days work. In the foreground is the winch for the lifting barriers on the top level crossing. (V. Mitchell).

1.13. In a sylvan setting, Henschel 0-6-0T no. 99 6102-0 departs from Alexisbad with a special vintage train from Nordhausen to Gernrode on 22nd May 2004. (J.F.Organ).

1.14. An example of the under utilisation of the powerful 2-10-2Ts on the former GHE route during the latter days of DR operation and the early period of HSB ownership. No.99 7245-6 pauses at Silberhütte hauling a lightweight train on 15th August 1992. (B. Benn).

1.15. Former Langeoog railcar no. 187 011-2 passes Mallet no. 99 5906-5 at Strassberg on 16th October 2002. The railcar was operating a service train to Gernrode whilst the Mallet was hauling the special train to Hasselfelde. (J. Marsh).

1.16.   No. 99 5906-5 departs from Strassberg with the special train. The rolling stock is part of the vintage set retained by the HSB and is painted in the traditional green livery. (J. Marsh).

1.17.   Stiege is the junction for three routes and this 1996 northward view has in the background the end of the balloon-shaped loop. The crisp dry snow was firm under foot, unlike most British deposits. (V. Mitchell).

1.18.   Diesel Hydraulic Co-Co no. 199 874-9 hauls a ballast train around the turning circle at Stiege on 16th October 2002. These former standard gauge machines were originally intended to replace steam haulage on the Harz system. Never popular locomotives, the few remaining examples are now restricted to use on works trains and the occasional freight. (J. Marsh).

1.19.   Mallet no. 99 5906-5 replenishes its water tanks at Hasselfelde whilst 2-10-2T no.99 7244-9 is seen on static display in the single road engine shed on 16th October 2002. (S. Sedgwick).

2. Nordhausen Wernigerode Eisenbahn.

Following many years of complicated negotiations, the concession to build a 61km railway across the spine of the Harz Mountains, linking Nordhausen and Wernigerode, was eventually approved in March 1896. Also involved in the scheme was a 19km branch from Drei Annen Hohne to the Brocken, with an upper station at an altitude of 1125m, a mere 17 metres below the summit. Construction of the metre gauge line began at both ends of the system with the first section from Nordhausen to Ilfeld being opened in July 1897. Two years later saw the whole route completed, opening up the hitherto remote area for freight and passenger services. A delay was caused by a dispute with some owners of requisitioned land at Wernigerode. As a result, track that had already been laid had to taken up whilst the problem was resolved. Consequently the track was ultimately relaid on a slightly different course to that originally used.

Originally the headquarters of the NWE were based at Nordhausen, where traffic figures had shown a continual increase. However much of this originated from the northern end of the line, where the workshops and main depot were situated. Consequently the operating headquarters were transferred to Wernigerode in 1916 in order to concentrate all aspects of the organisation in one area. Ten years later a new locomotive workshop was constructed at Wernigerode Westerntor in view of the limited space available at the terminus situated alongside the main line station. Other developments during the early years of the network were the aforementioned line connecting the GHE at Stiege with the NWE at Eisfelder Talmühle in 1905, whilst in 1913 a connection with the Südharzeisenbahn branch to Tanne was created at Sorge being principally used for through carriages between Braunlage, Wernigerode and the Brocken.

The NWE continued to provide a healthy traffic during the inter-war years. Whilst a combination of freight and passenger services were the major source of revenue for the main route between Wernigerode and Nordhausen, the Brocken branch was almost solely dependent upon tourist traffic for its continued existence. Despite a number of setbacks which could have had more serious effects, such as a strike by workers in 1920 followed by another the following year, plus a landslide in 1927 which washed away an embankment, these were overcome without any substantial loss of business. The landslide had serious repercussions in that a mixed train plunged into the empty void resulting in the death of four staff and two passengers. The 1930s saw many improvements to the permanent way with many of the tighter curves being re-aligned with a less severe radius in order to increase the line speed. The NWE's first railcar was introduced in 1936 for use on lighter accelerated services, following the successful introduction of a smaller machine by the GHE in 1933. Unlike the GHE railcar, the NWE's "T1" could haul up to three carriages on the grades to the Brocken summit. It was so successful that two further railcars were ordered but they were not delivered until 1940. The later "T2" and "T3" were effectively diesel locomotives, the passenger seating being replaced by a luggage compartment. A turbocharger added to the power unit resulted in an increased performance, which allowed them to haul four carriages.

The outbreak of war in 1939 saw a dramatic change in the fortunes of the system. With fuel shortages and travelling restrictions, it was the military traffic that kept the railway alive. This had a sinister side to its operations in that during the later years of the conflict, underground factories used in the production of V2 rockets were established near Nordhausen and Steinerne Renne, the latter heavily disguised in the forests between Wernigerode and Drei Annen Hohne. A 2.5km connection to a PoW camp at Harzungen was laid in 1944 from Niedersachswerfen Ost and dismantled again in 1947.

With the onset of peace in 1945, the NWE network, along with the GHE, was located just inside the border of the Soviet sector. As mentioned previously, the majority of the GHE was dismantled and shipped to Russia whilst the NWE was considered to be important enough to be retained by the new regime. Consequently a passenger service was re-instated between Wernigerode and Nordhausen by October of that year, although the Brocken branch remained closed.

Following the creation of the German Democratic Republic on October 7th 1949, the NWE effectively ceased to exist and became part of Deutsche Reichsbahn, the transfer actually taking place on January 1st 1950. In an attempt to gain international recognition, the GDR organised a Winter Sports event at Schierke during February 1950, which entailed reopening the lower section of the Brocken line for passenger traffic. From May 1950 a limited service up to the summit station was re-introduced, the first since the end of the war. After 1952 all passengers were required to be issued with a special pass, whilst a respectable tourist traffic developed again throughout the 1950s although not with the same flair as that established pre-war. Unfortunately this was all to end on 13th August 1961 with the sealing of the border between the two halves of Germany. Only supply trains ran to serve the increasing establishment of military hardware on the summit of the Brocken.

During the period of DR control, much investment was put into the Harz system in order to provide an integrated transport system. In addition to improvements to the infrastructure, new powerful steam locomotives, based on a 1930 design, were purchased in 1954 whilst diesel powered motive power was introduced in 1988 principally for freight haulage. The handling of freight traffic was streamlined from 1961 by the introduction of braked transporter wagons for standard gauge stock, thus eliminating the transhipment of goods between standard and narrow gauge wagons. The earlier, un-braked, transporter vehicles continued to be used to carry standard gauge wagons in the environs of Wernigerode and Nordhausen, where the gradients were less steep. From 1979 weighted points were installed in many stations to simplify crossing procedures whilst radio signalling was introduced in the following year.

Due to a combination of poor roads and the limited amount of private car ownership in the GDR, the railways played an important role in the daily transport needs of that country. The situation in West Germany was very different with the DB main line railways being modernised to a very high standard whilst minor routes, including the majority of narrow gauge systems, were closed and replaced by road transport. The DR railways in the East continued to operate much as they had for decades and were regarded as a working museum piece as a consequence.

Following the fall of the Iron Curtain in 1989 and the reunification of Germany in 1990, it was obvious that many changes would follow. The most significant event as far as the Harz area was concerned was the closure and dismantling of the Soviet "listening post" and associated military presence on the Brocken summit. Following the withdrawal of the Soviet authorities, the upper reaches of the mountain were declared an area of outstanding scenic and scientific attraction, known as the Hochharz National Park. Calls to reopen the upper section, which reached the DR authorities in December 1989, did not fall on deaf ears. One group instrumental in channelling these efforts was the Interessengemeinschaft Harzer Schmalspur-und Brockenbahn.e.V. (IG-HSB or Harz Railways Society). This society was set up and organised largely by the local railwaymen to cater for the best interests and their employees. They developed a transport policy for the Harz region, which was largely adopted by DR and the states of Sächsen-Anhalt and Thüringen. The society was able to assist effectively in fighting off a West German bid to close the whole system apart from the Brocken line, which would have been retained using modern railcars.

The upper section of the Brocken line above Schierke was reopened for passenger trains on 15th September 1991, following the many years of closure and relaying the worst stretches of track. Interestingly the driver of the first public special train was the same driver of the last passenger train in 1961! After completion of the rebuilding work, a full service was resumed from 1st July 1992. However, this was only achieved after a major battle with environmental groups who tried to stop the line reopening. Their reasoning was that large parts of the Brocken had remained completely undisturbed due to access being forbidden as a result of the military activities at the summit. Consequently a large area had reverted to nature which the environmentalists wanted to preserve. A compromise was reached whereby visitors must keep to the relatively few marked paths near the summit and not enter the nature reserve area.

Deutsche Reichsbahn (DR) and Deutsche Bundesbahn (DB) were amalgamated into a new Deutsche Bahn (German Railways) retaining the DB initials but with a new logo. During the same period, the Harz system, as recorded in the GHE section above, was privatised in 1993 to become known as the Harzer Schmalspurbahnen (HSB) with its headquarters in Wernigerode. As in the case of the former GHE route, the lines of the old NWE were divided into two sections for marketing purposes. These became Die Harzquerbahn (Railway crossing the Harz) for the Wernigerode to Nordhausen route whilst the branch from Drei Annen Hohne to the summit of the Brocken was named Die Brockenbahn. More recent investment by the HSB has been the upgrading of the main stations, particularly on the Nordhausen and Hasselfelde routes, whilst full signalling has been installed on the Wernigerode to Brocken section to maximise capacity and safety.

Since the late 1990s there have typically been eleven steam hauled return services daily on the Brocken line between April and October, with a slight reduction during the winter months. There are currently four connections over the Harzquerbahn between Wernigerode and Nordhausen each day although only one steam hauled service now originates in Nordhausen. This operates to the Brocken in summer and through to Wernigerode during the winter. A further steam hauled service runs from Wernigerode to Eisfelder Talmühle and return.

The 61km journey from Wernigerode to Nordhausen is one of many contrasts. The terminal station at Wernigerode is situated alongside the main line station, which is served by the Hannover to Leipzig route. The metre gauge station consists of three roads serving a single faced platform and an island platform with an additional loop line between the two platform roads. Between the narrow gauge and standard gauge lines are situated the metre gauge sidings and turntable, which lead to a modern concrete three road locomotive shed completed in 1990. The sidings are dominated by a large signal box and shed master's office of particularly austere appearance, alongside which are a coal stage and watering facilities. The HSB

have recently constructed an elevated viewing platform alongside the principal platform from which commanding views of the station area and locomotive servicing depot can be obtained.

Leaving the station, the line crosses a busy main road before reaching the more centrally positioned Westerntor station, near to the historic centre of the beautifully preserved town. This was the original northern terminus of the line, the extension to the current terminus alongside the main line station was not constructed until the late 1930s. Alongside the station is situated the large workshop complex, which was built in 1926, together with carriage sidings plus additional locomotive sheds. Almost immediately after Westerntor, the single line crosses a small river followed by a busy level crossing at a major road junction on the outskirts of the town. Following a stretch of line running behind the southern outskirts of Wernigerode, there follows a section of street running at Kirchstrasse (Church Street) where the large locomotives almost touch the old wooden framed buildings. After a small halt and passing loop at Hasserode, the line enters the forest on the lower slopes of the Harz Mountains. The next station at Steinerne Renne is approached via the sharpest curve on the system with a radius of 60 metres, which entails the route doubling back on itself. The line then climbs through the forest via innumerable curves and the only tunnel on any of the former East German narrow gauge systems. Shortly before Drei Annen Hohne, part of the forest has been cleared and the line climbs around reverse curves on a ledge before plunging back into the trees for the final climb to the junction. This cleared area is now re-growing rapidly as this is commercial woodland.

At Drei Annen Hohne, 15km from the northern terminus, locomotives take water whilst it is also a principal passing point on the system. It is quite normal for three trains to occupy the station at one time, bound for Nordhausen, Wernigerode and Brocken respectively. Originally there were two stations at Drei Annen Hohne, a disused subway at the northern end of the platform being the only surviving reminder. The other station served a standard gauge branch from the Halberstadt and Blankenburg line that closed in 1945, although the main line section of the route is still in operation. Leaving the station, the two routes join together for a short distance before separating to run parallel until the Brocken line veers off to the right to begin its long steep climb to the summit. The Nordhausen line continues in a southerly direction passing over an undulating route mainly on the edge of the forests. Between Elend and Sorge the route used to run alongside the Iron Curtain which was clearly visible as a high heavily defended steel fence amid an area of barren scrub. The route proceeds via Benneckenstein and Tiefenbachmühle until Eisfelder Talmühle is reached, where the Selketalbahn joins the former NWE line. The remaining 17km to Ilfeld and Nordhausen run through a more open landscape as the mountains recede into the distance. Shortly before Ilfeld is reached the line crosses a stone viaduct comprising of three arches, which is one of the most significant civil engineering structures on the line. The original viaduct collapsed in January 1948 due to severe flooding, following heavy snowfall, and took 18 months to rebuild. Services continued to operate each side of the damaged viaduct, passengers changing trains via a ten-minute detour on foot.

The southern terminus occupies a large site with numerous sidings and former industrial connections alongside the running line on the approach to the station, with its wide island platform. Adjacent to the narrow gauge station, the standard gauge station is situated, served by the Kassel to Leipzig route. During the Iron Curtain period, this line would of course have been severed, with Nordhausen being effectively a terminal station on the main line. The same also applied at Wernigerode where the Hannover route was closed in the proximity of the border near Bad Harzburg.

July 1913

WERNIGERODE and NORDHAUSEN.														
Wernigerode...dep	7a12	9a32	11a10	12p2	1p38	3p10	...		4p30	4p42	8p10		
Steinerne Renne	7 38	9 59	1134	1231	2 2	3 36	...		4 55	5 7	8 35		
Drei Annen–Hohne ...	8 0	10 20	1155	1252	2 23	...		4§p8	5 18	5 29	8 56		
Schierke	8 25	10§29	1214		2 41	...		4 23	5 50	...	...		
Brocken .... arr	9 8	11 20	1 0	...	3 25	...		5 4	6§31	...	...		
Elend (for Schierke)...	8 22	10 40	1214	...	2 43	...				5 48	9 14		
Sorge ....a.m.	8 43	11 0	1233	...	3 6	...	...		...	6 11	9 35		
Benneckstein ......5‡20	8 57	11 13		...	3 30	...	...		...	6 26	9 50		
Eisfelder 5 50	9 34	11 45	...	...	4 17	...	...		...	7 1	1028		
Netzkater............5 59	9 42	11 54	...	...	4 28	...	...		...	7 10	1037		
Nordhausen arr 6 37	1016	12 29	...	...	5 9	...	...			7 46	1115		
Nordhausen ......dep	6 a0	9a15	p.m.	2 p0	1p30	3p20	...		6c32	8*p10			
Netzkater..................	6 37	10 0	...	2 39	2 6	3 59	...		7 9	8 53			
Eisfelder	6 48	10 14	...	2 49	2 18	4 7	...		7 22	9 10			
Benneckstein	7 19	10 48	...		2 51	4 43	...		7 54	9 42			
Sorge	7 35	11 2	12 38	...	3 4	5 0	...		8 10	...			
Elend (for Schierke) ...	7 55	11 24	1 3	...	3 23	5 21	p.m.		8 33	...			
Brocken ....dep	7 §0	10 48	12 28	2 p0	...	4 30	6 §0		...	...			
Schierke	7§40	11 34	1 10	2 41	...	5 16	6 40		...	...			
Drei Annen–Hohne	8 10	11 55	1 26	2 56	3 42	5 50	6 55		8 56	...			
Steinerne Renne	8 31	12 18	1 48		4 3	6 14			9 19	...			
Wernigerode 166 arr	8 54	12 45	2 14	...	4 26	6 40	...		9 46	...			
*—Monday, Wednesday, and Friday only.														
‡—Sun., Tues., and Thurs. only. §—Runs until 31st August.														

2.1.   Due to its close proximity to the Iron Curtain, photographs of the Harz system during the period of the "cold war" were officially forbidden, particularly on the Wernigerode to Nordhausen route. However some scenes were recorded without attracting the attention of the authorities. One of the impressive 2-10-2Ts, no.99 7234-0, was preparing to leave the depot at Wernigerode on 15th April 1976. Note the austere signal box and double deck stock on the standard gauge line in the background. (K.Taylorson).

2.2.   Eighteen years later, Germany has been reunified and the Harz system privatised. Despite these dramatic changes the scene at Wernigerode depot has changed little as 2-10-2T no.99 7236-5 has its coal bunker replenished in February 1994. (J. Marsh).

2.3.   The impressive bulk of the LKM 2-10-2Ts can be appreciated in this view of no. 99 7243-1 receiving final preparations, before leaving the depot on 24th May 2004. (J.F. Organ).

2.4.   Normally based at Nordhausen, Henschel 0-6-0T no. 99 6101 was an unusual visitor to Wernigerode depot on 28th August 1995. (D.Trevor Rowe).

2.5.   Wernigerode depot has from left to right, 2-10-2T no. 99 7248-4, two Jung Mallets, restored with their original NWE numbers 11 and 13, plus 2-10-2T no.99 7236-5 outside the shed on a cold day in February 1994. (J. Marsh).

2.6.   Wernigerode station is seen in DR days when it still had that characteristic shabby appearance always associated with the railways of East Germany during the GDR period. 2-10-2T no. 99 7234-0 was viewed shunting stock alongside the central platform on 15th April 1976. (K.Taylorson).

2.7.   Another scene at Wernigerode station on the same occasion as 2-10-2T no.99 7238-1 prepares to depart with a train to Nordhausen. Despite the reported lack of investment in its railways by the GDR, the infrastructure appears to be in excellent condition. (K. Taylorson).

2.8.   Almost 20 years later, the same locomotive was about to haul another train from Wernigerode to Nordhausen. No. 99 7238-1 will soon depart with a train that included a Ffestiniog Travel party among its passengers on 18th October 1995. (J.F.Organ).

2.9.   Having just arrived with a special train from the Brocken, Jung 0-4-4-0T Mallets nos 99 5901 and 99 5902 were viewed being uncoupled from the rolling stock at Wernigerode station on 22nd May 2004. (J.F.Organ).

2.10. No. 99 7232-4 pulls away from the station at Wernigerode Westerntor on an Autumn day in 1990. The station was built in 1936, replacing the original terminus, after the line was extended to the new terminus alongside the standard gauge station. (J.F.Organ coll.)

2.11. 2-10-2T no. 99 7240-7 storms across the busy level crossing near Wernigerode Westerntor on 16th October 1995. Note the cobbled road surface, a legacy of the GDR. (J.F.Organ).

2.12. Shortly after the level crossing, no.99 7240-7 enters the section of reserved track at the southern end of Wernigerode on 28th August 1995. The car is parked on what is officially a footpath! (D.Trevor Rowe).

2.13. Approaching the halt at Wernigerode Kirchstrasse the Schwartzkopff 2-10-2T, when still running as 99 7222-5, passes behind the gardens of houses in this quiet suburb on the same occasion. (D.Trevor Rowe).

2.14. On a cold February day in 1994, no. 99 7236-5 enters the short section of street running at Kirchstrasse. The tarmac surface of the adjacent road appears to be in some need of attention. (J. Marsh).

2.15. The large 2-10-2T seems to almost touch the houses at the upper end of the Kirchstrasse as no. 99 7243-1 leaves the roadside section on 18th October 1995. Note the limited space for motor vehicles in the main street. (J.F.Organ).

2.16.   Shortly after Kirchstrasse is the chocolate factory at Hasserode. This was originally linked to the railway by a private siding until it was abandoned in 2002. The last train to leave the factory was hauled by Henschel 0-6-0T no. 99 6101 on 18th October 2002. (S.Sedgwick).

2.17.   No. 99 7238-1 eases through the tortuous curves at Steinerre Renne with a Brocken bound train on 18th October 2002. The passing loop is controlled by automatic spring loaded points, the station building being normally unmanned. (J.Marsh).

2.18.   Mallet no.13 hauls a tradzüg train comprised of vintage rolling stock around the reverse curves, where the forest had been cleared north of Drei Annen Hohne, on 2nd July 1994. (B.Benn).

→

2.19   Drie Annen Hohne is the junction for the Brocken line and it required much labour with shovels to keep it operational on 22nd February 1996. Few passengers complained, as winter sports were their main objective. (V. Mitchell).

→

2.20.   A characteristically busy period recorded at Drei Annen Hohne. No 99 7238-1 was replenishing its water before attacking the climb to the Brocken whilst no.99 7233-2 arrives with a Nordhausen train on 17th October 1995. (J.F.Organ).

→

2.21.   The modern image of the HSB as used for the lighter services. DB Halberstadt railcar no. 187 018-1 and the prototype unit no. 187 015-3 were recorded at Drei Annen Hohne with a service train from Nordhausen to Wernigerode on 24th May 2004. (J.F.Organ).

2.22. Although rarely seen on passenger trains in recent years, former standard gauge Diesel-Hydraulic Co-Co no. 199 874-9 was double heading with 2-10-2T no. 99 7236-5 in order to return to its base at Nordhausen, following maintenance at Wernigerode Westerntor workshops. The powerful combination was recorded departing from Drei Annen Hohne on 24th May 2004. (J.F.Organ).

2.23. No. 99 7245-6 was viewed taking water at Eisfelder Talmühle whilst hauling a freight train to Nordhausen. Note the characteristic large half-timber framed station building dominating this scene recorded on 18th October 2002. (J.Marsh).

2.24. The large southern terminus of the Harz system is located at Nordhausen, overlooked by buildings of typical German architecture. The line with the fresh ballast to the left of the photograph is the new connection to the town tram system. Some modern trams are thus able to run north to Ilfeld. Henschel 0-6-0T no.99 6101 was viewed shunting the stock of a short mixed train on 18th October 2002. (S.Sedgwick).

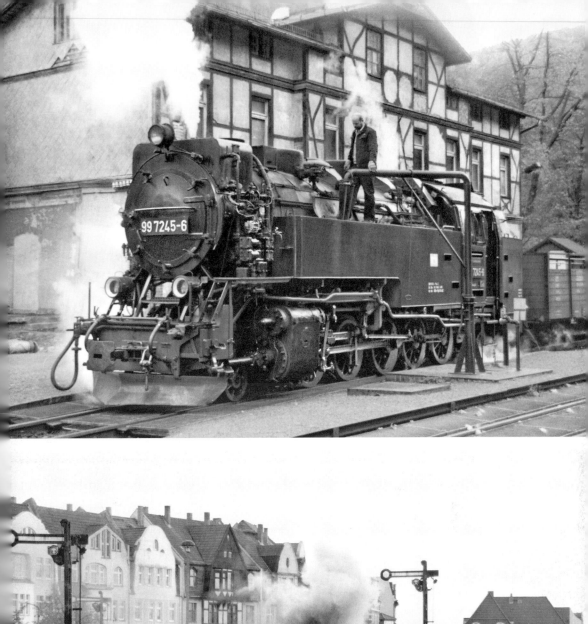

2.25   A view in the other direction six years earlier shows no. 99 7231-6 shunting the sidings before their alteration. In the distance is a level crossing and the signal box is on the left. (V. Mitchell).

2.26.   The recently constructed interchange station with the Nordhausen tram system receives diesel railcars via the link shown in picture 2.24. The prototype railcar built at Wittenberge in 1996, no. 187 015-3, was viewed alongside a tram on 18th October 2002. The original terminus is in the centre backround. (S.Sedgwick).

3. Brockenbahn

The Brocken line, after diverting from the Nordhausen route at Drei Annen Hohne, begins a gruelling 19km climb on an almost unbroken ruling gradient of 1 in 30. Much of the first part of the climb to the intermediate station at Schierke is through dense forest. Following a brief stop, the climb continues through more plantations of pine forest around the very sharp curve at Ecklerloch, where the nature reserve begins, to Goetheweg the site of a former halt. Now it consists of a siding into which descending trains are directed in order to allow an ascending train to pass unhindered during the busy timetable period. Once the line is clear, the descending train is propelled from the siding to regain the main line. At Goethemoor the line is once again running alongside the former border, now an attractive scenic footpath through the Hochharz National Park. The final part of the climb, above the tree line, involves an almost complete circuit of the upper reaches of the mountain before the upper terminus is reached at 1125m. The former highly sensitive military installations at the summit have been transformed into a weather station, a radio and television transmitter and a museum. The former barracks now house a welcoming restaurant and bar with outdoor terraces where one can enjoy refreshments in the clear mountain air, at least when the weather is kind! During the winter months, whilst trains continue to run, the conditions at the summit can be very hostile. Most winter days sees the summit above the cloud base with visibility below 50 metres and often with extremely high winds.

The Brocken area is rich in folklore and was in fact the setting for Goethe's Faust and its celebrated Walpurgisnacht scene featuring witches and devils. The passing of winter is celebrated each year on April 30th with Walpurgis Night when the local population dress accordingly for an evening of high spirits on the Brocken. During the years of inaccessibility to the summit, these celebrations were held at Schierke, which still plays a major part in the occasion. However, since the reopening of the entire Brocken line, highly decorated special trains with equally decorated passengers ascend the line to the summit where the passing of winter is celebrated in style.

3.1.   A classic scene at Drei Annen Hohne, where no. 99 222 was recorded making a spirited departure with a Brocken bound train, at the point where the two routes diverge, on 18th October 2002. The Nordhausen line is seen in the foreground. (S.Sedgwick).

3.2.   Storming the Brocken as no. 99 7233-2 ⟶
commences the long climb to the summit. Apart
from a brief respite at Schierke, the locomotive
faces an almost continual 19km ascent at 1 in 30.
This scene was recorded on 17th October 1995.
(J.F.Organ).

3.3   Three photographs of the intermediate
station at Schierke from 22nd February 1996
highlight the operating problems that can occur
on the mountain line. Clearance work resulted in
snow elbow deep. (V. Mitchell).

⟶
3.4.   Icicles on the station reflected good roof insulation, but those on the coaches indicated
inadequate heating. The tiny steam heaters therein were usually barely warm; the toilets have no
S-bends to freeze - practical, but draughty. (V. Mitchell).

3.5   One of the giant diesel locomotives propelled the rotary snow plough to the summit before the first train was due to arrive. (V. Mitchell).

3.6.   Following a signal stop at Goetheweg whilst waiting for a down train to enter the siding, no. 99 7238-1 blasts away up the 1 in 30 gradient towards the Brocken summit. This view was recorded from the balcony of the last coach of the down train on 23rd May 2004. The gradient is too steep for a loop and so a siding is provided. (J.F.Organ).

3.7. 2-10-2T no. 99 7235-7 on the upper section of the gruelling climb. This view at Goethemoor on 3rd May 1995 shows the recently constructed footpath through the Hochharz National Park, which is very near to the former border between East and West Germany. (B.Benn).

3.8. After the arrival of the train seen in 3.4, the fireman had to set about unblocking the points, despite the recent passage of the train shown in 3.5. Ice-clad on the left is a modern restaurant for tourists. (V. Mitchell).

3.9. The points having been freed, no. 99 7236-5 ran round its train and the other passenger used the photographer's camera to record him under the icicles. They were not likely to move at minus 14 centigrade. The snow was being blown horizontally by an easterly gale and thus conditions were not ideal for skiing. *Inset* - On the ascent, all brake blocks became coated with ice rendering them useless for the descent. Much hammering was needed, with collars upturned. (V. Mitchell).

3.10. Jung 0-4-4-0T Mallet no. 99 5901 has just arrived at Brocken station with a special from Wernigerode. Shortly after this photograph was recorded on 23rd May 2004, a brief heavy blizzard reduced visibility to zero whilst the locomotive shunted the stock into the adjacent siding. The large construction in the background is part of the former Soviet military establishment, now used as a weather station. (J.F.Organ).

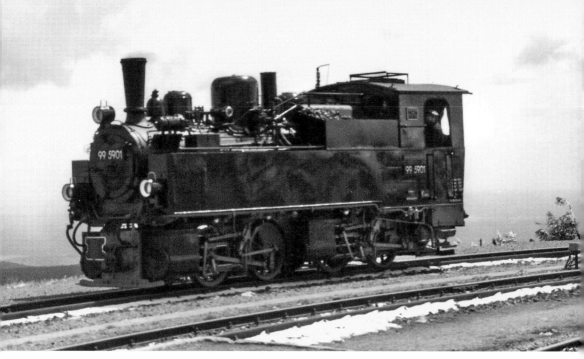

3.11.   Seemingly "on top of the world" no. 99 5901 completes its shunting manoeuvres after the blizzard had passed and the sun reappeared. Such weather conditions are unusual for that time of year, although the railway continues to operate throughout the winter months when the summit is permanently covered in deep snow. (J.F.Organ).

3.12.   No. 99 7243-1 prepares to depart from the 1125m high Brocken terminus on 17th October 1995. Another part of the former military hardware can be seen above the cab roof, this having now been adapted as the local radio and television transmitter. (J.F.Organ).

4. Locomotives and Rolling Stock in the Harz

The first locomotives to work on both the GHE and NWE were modest 0-4-0Ts and 0-6-0Ts, supplied by Mecklenburgische Waggonfabrik of Güstrow and Henschel of Kassel respectively. Whilst these small locomotives were adequate for the former line, the long steep gradients, excessive curvature and higher traffic levels of the NWE required something more powerful and flexible. Consequently, between 1897 and 1901 twelve 0-4-4-0T compound Mallets were purchased. These were all the products and design of Arnold Jung, apart from three supplied by Gustrower Locomotiv-und Waggonfabrik under sub contract in 1897. They were fitted with inside frames on the front, low pressure, bogie and outside frames on the rigid high pressure rear section, with an axle loading of nine tonnes. Six of these excellent locomotives were requisitioned for war service in France during World War 1, from which they never returned, whilst three of the remaining survivors are still in service. These were formerly NWE nos 11,12 and 13, their DR numbers being 99 5901-6, 99 5902-4 and 99 5903-2. Two of the Mallets, nos 11 and 13, were restored to their original green livery and NWE numbers following the formation of the HSB and are regularly seen hauling vintage trains on special occasions. During a recent overhaul, no.11 reverted to its DR livery and identification of 99 5901 whilst 99 5902 has also received similar treatment.

As compensation for the locomotives lost during the war, the Army supplied three surplus locomotives following the end of hostilities. These included two 0-6-0Ts built in 1914 by Henschel that had been commissioned to compare the benefits of superheated and saturated steam. Thanks to the efforts of two supporting societies, these are still in service as nos 99 6101-2 and 99 6102-0, being known affectionately as "Pfiffi" and "Fiffi" respectively, the former of which is the superheated example. Their NWE numbers were 6 and 7. The third locomotive supplied by the Army was another 0-4-4-0T Mallet, built in 1918 by Maschinenbau-Gesellschaft of Karlsruhe, being numbered 41 by the NWE. Much the same size as the Jung machines, this proved to be a popular locomotive and is still

in regular service on the HSB (Selketalbahn) as no. 99 5906-5. It was almost not so lucky having been sold, illegally, by DR to the Deutscher Eisenbahn-Verein (DEV), a long established museum line near Bremen. DR had no right to sell the locomotive as the railway and its stock was subject to a preservation order! A court order prevented its removal from Wernigerode at the beginning of 1991. The dispute was resolved in 1995 when DB, as successors to DR, acquired another similar Karlsruhe Mallet from the Albtalbahn in Bavaria which was donated to DEV.

Other locomotives that worked on the system at various periods during the inter-war years included a pair of unsuitable Henschel 2-8-2Ts for a short time, plus two Orenstein & Koppel 0-6-6-0T Mallets which were too heavy for the track and sold in 1921 to a Bolivian tin mine. Finally two rather more successful 2-4-4-2T Mallets built by Borsig in 1922 and 1923 were supplied principally for use on the Brocken line. These survived until 1959, after the newly acquired 2-10-2Ts had proved themselves. One was transferred to the Gera line in Thüringen where it was found to be too heavy. Both locomotives were scrapped at Görlitz works in 1966 and 1967. Another interesting machine that was in the care of DR and the HSB temporarily during the 1990s, although not in use, was a compound Fairlie double engine built by SMF Hartmann of Chemnitz. This locomotive, dating from 1902, was on loan from the Dresden Transport Museum and normally resided in the depot at Ilfeld. Unusually it has features normally associated with a tram locomotive, including a continuous full-length cab roof and enclosed motion. Along with two sister Fairlies, it had originally been supplied for use on a short line between Reichenbach and Oberheinsdorf in Saxony that included an extensive section of street running. In the late 1990s it was moved back to Oberheinsdorf to be displayed in a small museum. An offer by the HSB to return it to working order was turned down by the Transport Museum on the grounds that too much of the original fabric of the locomotive would be destroyed in the process.

In 1939 two 2-6-2Ts were ordered from Krupp, one each for the NWE and GHE, which were intended to be the prototypes of a standard class of locomotive for both lines. Due to the outbreak of war, only one was completed which was supplied to the NWE where it became their no.21. This powerful compact machine proved to be an excellent engine in service. Had Germany not been so drastically divided in the post war years, other examples would almost certainly have been supplied. This locomotive is normally based at Gernrode for use on the Selketalbahn and in 1991 it was restored to its original NWE green livery and number to work with the vintage stock following their conversion to air braking. During a major overhaul in 1994 it reverted to its DR number of 99 6001-4 and black livery.

The locomotives most associated with the Harz system are the massive 2-10-2Ts. The history of these impressive locomotives began in 1930 when Schwartzkopff built three locomotives for use on the Eisfeld to Schönbrunn line, south of the Harz near Erfurt. These successful machines, fitted with the same boiler as standard gauge class 81 locomotives, were highly suited to the haulage of heavy freight trains on the steep gradients through the Thüringen forests. During World War 2, two of these locomotives were drafted to the Thamshavn-Lökken railway in Norway, their subsequent fate being unknown. The lone survivor remained at Eisfeld and was used as a prototype for a new improved version ordered by DR from VEB Locomotivbrau "Karl Marx"at Babelsberg (LKM). Improvements to the original design included welded boilers and plate frames, Krauss-Helmholtz leading and trailing pony trucks and limited articulation between the first and second coupled axles was later added by the use of Beugniot levers. This was a modernised version of the system applied to the successful "Feldbahn" 0-8-0Ts during World War One. A total of 17 Neubau or new build locomotives were constructed between 1954 and 1956. Four were sent to Eisfeld to join the pioneer no.99 222 whilst the remaining 13 arrived at Wernigerode. It became immediately apparent that the locomotives, as built, could not negotiate the sharpest curves. Only after the addition of the Beugniot levers and fitting wider un-flanged tyres to the centre pair of driving wheels could successful operation be ensured. Once these and other less serious "teething troubles" were resolved, the locomotives have subsequently been very successful on the difficult and varied routes through the Harz. After a life of 50 years, these machines are still referred to as the "new build" locomotives!

When the Eisfeld line closed in 1973, the five 2-10-2Ts based there, including the original 1930 built locomotive, were transferred to Wernigerode where they joined their hard working sister engines. Shortly after arriving at its new home, no.99 222 was overhauled and rebuilt incorporating many of the modifications incorporated in the later locomotives. During the final years of the DR, all their locomotives were renumbered with a prefix in front of the individual number. Thus the original no.99 222 became 99 7222 whilst the later engines, which originally carried the numbers 99 231 - 99 247, were changed to 99 7231 - 99 7247. In addition each engine carries a different suffix number which is used in conjunction with a computerised system. As can be seen from the accompanying photographs, these suffix numbers have no apparent logical sequence, no doubt they mean something to someone! For instance the original 1930 locomotive was 99 7222-5 whilst one of the later machines is now 99 7246-4. The last of these powerful engines no. 99 7247-2 reverted to its old number of 99 247 late in 1990 and is the only member of the class to be still fitted with a vacuum brake ejector. Following a recent overhaul, the pioneer 99 7222-5 also reverted to its original number of 99 222.

Shortly before the formation of HSB in 1993, the old DR and DB organisations had merged into the new Deutsche Bahn. At this time the Harz locomotives were allocated DB numbers in the 099 series, however these were never carried. Following their transfer to HSB ownership, the locomotives retained their former DR numbers.

Compared to the handsome Mallets of earlier vintage, these large locomotives are in a completely different league. They are very impressive machines, indeed they are the most powerful metre gauge locomotives in Europe producing a power output of 700hp, but they are certainly not handsome! The superheated boilers are fitted with an array of domes, for both steam and sanding purposes, whilst there is a complex variety of external plumbing. A large air brake compressor and feed water pump is fitted along each side of the smokebox whilst the pre-heater (direct mixing type) for the latter is situated in a rectangular housing mounted on top of the smokebox, directly in front of the chimney. This results in a very blunt appearance to the frontal aspect of these huge machines, which are larger than many standard gauge locomotives. Following its major overhaul and rebuild in 1999, no. 99 222 has been restored as much as possible to its original appearance including a tubular feed water heater (indirect surface type) above the smokebox, replacing the rectangular housing fitted to the later LKM built examples.

Originally they were acquired for heavy freight haulage, for which they were eminently suitable. However since reunification, this traffic has become almost negligible, diesel locomotives handling the limited amount of surviving freight haulage. The HSB operation is principally a passenger carrying line and the 2-10-2Ts are usefully employed hauling fully laden eight coach trains from Wernigerode and Nordhausen to the Brocken. Due to this they have earned the unofficial name of "Brocken Loks". On the Selketalbahn it was a different story with the large locomotives somewhat under employed hauling three coach trains on that section of the system. Consequently economic sense has prevailed with the Karlsruhe Mallet and the 2-6-2T normally based at Gernrode, working alongside the railcars, although they are often seen hauling special trains over the entire network. The two 0-6-0Ts are based at Nordhausen or Gernrode where they are maintained by the supporting societies. However, these are also occasionally used on special workings throughout the system.

During the fuel crisis of the 1970s, which seriously affected the GDR, most of the 2-10-2Ts were converted to oil firing between 1976 and 1981. Considering that one of their major roles during this period was haulage of coal trains to the power station at Silberhütte, this unpopular and poorly conceived conversion

was particularly poignant. One locomotive that escaped this modernisation was the pioneer 99 7222-5, which at that time was employed as a stationary heating unit at Westerntor works in order to keep the operating locomotives warm overnight. Following the increase in crude oil prices in the early 1980s, DR decreed that oil firing would no longer be permitted. An exception was made for the Harz locomotives until they could be converted back to coal firing, which was completed in 1984. As oil burners the "7" in the running number was replaced by a "0".

Of this fleet of eighteen 2-10-2Ts, seven are currently "mothballed" as a strategic reserve. Most are stored at Wernigerode Westerntor works whilst some are located at other locations throughout the system. The latter include no.99 7244-9 at Hasselfelde, which was withdrawn from service with a cracked cylinder, and 99 247 which is stored at Gernrode.

Originally vacuum braking had been used on the Harz system. DR found it increasingly difficult to source or produce spare parts and consequently converted all the stock to air braking between 1982 and 1990, the last set of carriages to be converted being the vintage or "oldtimer" set.

In the case of the 2-10-2Ts, 2-6-2T and the Henschel 0-6-0Ts, this was a fairly easy conversion as they were already fitted with dual braking systems. However the earlier Mallets carried no such refinements. At first it seemed that the days of the Mallets were numbered but the supporting society acquired and installed an air pump to 99 5903 in 1992. The other Mallets were subsequently modified whilst receiving major overhauls during the mid-1990s, the engineers successfully fitted the air brake compressors inside a special compartment incorporated into one of the water tanks. Consequently the outward appearance of these vintage machines was unaffected by these modifications, although a small amount of water capacity was sacrificed in the process.

Diesel power made its first appearance in the Harz when the GHE acquired a railcar in 1933. This 4 wheeled vehicle, with a seating capacity of 25, was built by Waggonfabrik Dessau and was numbered T1. The success of this railcar, which is still in service, led to the NWE placing an order for a 23 seat bogie railcar in 1936, following trials the previous year with a similar machine built by Wismar which was destined for use in Venezuela. The new NWE railcar was built by Maschinenfabrik Augsburg-Nürnberg (MAN) and was intended for use on a high-speed service to the Brocken. Two diesel-electric railcars with a large parcel and luggage capacity were ordered from Wismar in 1938, although they were not delivered until 1940. These powerful Triebwagen, fitted with the same MAN diesel engines as fitted to the German Navy U Boats, could haul four passenger coaches and were obviously very useful until wartime fuel shortages forced their temporary retirement. One of these, NWE no.T3, has survived into HSB service. T1 received the DR number 187 001 whilst T3 became 187 025.

In 1988 Deutsche Reichsbahn had a surplus of Bo-Bo centre cab standard gauge diesel hydraulic locomotives. It was intended to convert 30 of these to metre gauge and replace steam on the surviving DR metre gauge systems, which by that time was restricted to the Harz. In the event only ten were adapted and transferred. The conversion involved replacing the standard gauge four wheeled bogies with six wheeled metre gauge units, thus making them Co-Co machines. Towering above the rolling stock with their faded red livery, they soon gained the nickname of Rotkamels (Red Camels) and became despised and hated by enthusiasts. Although intended for freight haulage, they have also been seen hauling passenger trains on many occasions. Numbered in the 199xxx series, they were built by VEB Lokbau Henningsdorf between 1976 and 1978.

The intended replacement of steam power by these diesel hydraulic machines never came to fruition and the two types of motive power worked alongside each other harmoniously during the early years of the HSB era. With the emphasis on tourist traffic during the more recent past, for which the steam locomotives are one of the major attractions, the role of the diesel machines has diminished. Consequently only three remain in service, being used either on carriage shunting at Wernigerode, engineering

trains or the ballast traffic from the stone quarries near Eisfelder Talmühle. Another reason for their removal from passenger train haulage was due to excessive track wear as a result of their weight and the three axle bogies. All three remaining examples are equipped with radio remote control to enable the driver to double up as shunter.

More recent acquisitions were three railcars from the system on the island of Langeoog, off the North Sea coast of Germany, which arrived in 1995. These lightweight units, which had been displaced by new diesel locomotives at Langeoog, were successfully employed on off peak services between Gernrode, Harzgerode and Hasselfelde. Although principally at work on the former GHE section, they also operate on other parts of the system, particularly between Nordhausen and Ilfeld.

In 1996 a prototype railcar of modern design by the DB works at Wittenberge was supplied, followed by four production vehicles to a different design from DB Halberstadt in 1999. At Nordhausen a connection has been created with the town tram system, enabling through running from the HSB with the railcars to the tram stop in the main station forecourt. A casualty of the introduction of dual system trams (overhead electric or diesel) in early 2004 to the southern end of the system is the replacement of the early morning steam hauled school train between Nordhausen and Ilfeld. These dual system "Combino-Duo" trams run from the town tram network onto HSB metals as far as Ilfeld interspersed between the HSB railcar and steam services.

Passenger rolling stock consists of a fleet of bogie coaches with end balconies, so typical of most European narrow gauge railways. Originally they were painted plain green, although not such a drab shade as that used on much of the German standard gauge stock. Their standardised appearance, a result of two waves of DR modernisation during the 1970s and 80s, hides the fact that many carriages have their origins in original NWE or former Saxon vehicles. In an attempt to improve its image from 1973, DR repainted the majority in an attractive red and ivory livery. This colour scheme has been perpetuated by the HSB, although they have retained some of the older vehicles in the original green livery for the historic special trains (Taditionszüg) that operate at regular intervals on the system. The majority of passenger trains include a luggage van in their formation. These are either four wheeled or bogie vehicles and are painted plain red rather than the two-tone livery of the passenger stock.

At the time of reunification, freight traffic consisted of standard gauge wagons carried on transporter wagons. These consist of two basic types, rollwagen or rollböcke. The former consists of a bogie wagon with a low slung girder framed chassis, the main girders being set at standard gauge. The latter are simply narrow gauge bogies fitted with a cradle, which support the axles of the standard gauge wagons. Although offering a much easier transhipment system, the rollwagen system has the disadvantage of being much heavier to haul and consequently can restrict the number of vehicles that can be carried on one train. In 1997 modern air braked "Vevey System" rollböcke were introduced at Nordhausen, replacing the rollwagen. With the new system bogie standard gauge wagons can be carried and the loading and unloading of the wagons can be accomplished very quickly with the minimum of personnel.

Expansions into the 21st Century.

The recent developments at Nordhausen, where the HSB tracks have been extended to connect with the municipal tram system, have been mentioned above. Even more exciting extensions are planned at Gernrode during 2004. With DB having closed its unprofitable branch between Quedlinburg and Aschersleben, this has left Gernrode without a main line connection. With financial assistance from local government, the 9km standard gauge route between Gernrode and Quedlinburg is to be converted to metre gauge, providing the HSB with an extension to the historic medieval town and a connection with the DB system.

On the locomotive front, 2-10-2T no.99 7232 has been comprehensively rebuilt at Meiningen works. This work including the fitting of a completely new set of frames to an improved specification which were designed by the HSB workshops at Wernigerode. This could well be the beginning of a new generation of steam locomotives with virtually new machines being produced from the basic components of the original unit.

At Wernigerode a purpose built carriage works is to be constructed shortly, on the site of the old timber yard a short distance from Westerntor works. This will incorporate facilities for maintenance, cleaning and storage, allowing the stock to be kept under cover as much as possible.

With such positive developments, the Harz railway system is assured of a secure future.

4.1.   The oldest surviving locomotives still working on the HSB are the Jung 0-4-4-0T Mallets dating from 1897, of which three have been preserved. During the period they were restored to their original NWE numbers and green livery, nos 11 and 13 were recorded outside Wernigerode depot in February 1994. During a recent overhaul, no. 11 has been restored to the later black livery and former DR number of 99 5901 whilst no. 13 was stored out of use at Westerntor works awaiting overhaul. (J. Marsh).

4.2.   The M.G.Karlsruhe 0-4-4-0T Mallet dating from 1918, was supplied after World War 1 as compensation for requisitioned machines lost in France.   Originally NWE no.41, it has been restored to its DR condition and number 99 5906-5 and was photographed at Alexisbad on 22nd May 2004. (J.F.Organ).

4.3.   Also supplied as compensation after World War 1 were the two Henschel 0-6-0Ts built in 1914. Known affectionately as "Pfiffi" and "Fiffi", the former being superheated and the latter saturated. "Pfiffi", no. 99 6101, was seen replenishing its small water tanks at Alexisbad whilst hauling a demonstration freight train to Gernrode on 22nd May 2004. (J.F.Organ).

4.4.   No.99 6102-0 "Fiffi", the saturated 0-6-0T was also recorded at Alexisbad on the same occasion. Note that this version of the Henschel design has longer side tanks than its sister locomotive. (J.F.Organ).

4.5.   The Krupp 2-6-2T, dating from 1939, is normally based at Gernrode from where it works to Harzgerode and Hasselfelde. It was recorded departing from Alexisbad with a train bound for Hasselfelde in June 1996. (R.White - J.F.Organ. coll.)

4.6.   Restored largely to its original condition, the 1930 Schwartzkopff built 2-10-2T no.99 222 poses by the water crane at Drei Annen Hohne on 18th October 2002. Note the original type of circular reservoir for the feed water heater on the front of the smoke box. (J.Marsh).

4.7.   By contrast to the previous view, LKM built 2-10-2T no. 99 7245-6 was seen at the same location on 17th October 2002. The rectangular housing for the feed water heating equipment, which provides these locomotives with a rather blunt frontal appearance, is clearly shown in this view. (S.Sedgwick).

5. Metre Gauge lines in Thüringen

Reference has previously been made of the 32km Südharzeisenbahn and the 15km Eisfeld to Schönbrunn line in the Thüringen forests. In addition this area south of the Harz Mountains boasted another metre gauge line, the 25km route linking Gera and Wuitz-Mumsdorf to the south west of Leipzig.

Dating from 1899-1901, all three lines were quite different in character. The Südharzeisenbahn was principally a passenger carrying line whilst the Eisfeld line relied on the transport of timber for its major source of revenue. The Gera line was dependent upon the transport of lignite from the extensive mines in the area, the passenger traffic being mainly for the benefit of the miners employed at the pits.

Despite their contrasting traffic requirements, all three lines used similar types of locomotives during their years of operation. There were exceptions, the South Harz line was an early user of railcars for the majority of its passenger services whilst the Eisfeld line, as already noted, took delivery of the three original Schwartzkopff 2-10-2Ts in 1930. The lone survivor was joined by four of the later LKM versions in 1954. Both the South Harz and Gera line acquired Borsig 0-4-4-0T Mallets in 1899 and 1901 respectively, similar to the Jung examples in use on the NWE, whilst in 1922 Borsig supplied two 0-8-0Ts for use on the Gera to Wuitz-Mumsdorf route.

Common to all three lines were some interesting 0-10-0Ts supplied by Orenstein & Koppel in 1923. These decapods had the three central pairs of wheels connected by conventional coupling rods. However, the outer pairs were connected by means of Luttermöller internal gears, allowing limited articulation of the leading and trailing axles. O & K supplied three of these complex machines, principally for use on the Eisfeld line whilst in 1927 four more were constructed by Esslingen at Stuttgart. These later versions were more conventional machines, without the complexities of the Luttermöller geared axles, being originally supplied for use in the Baden area of southern Germany. Henschel had also supplied some conventional 0-10-0Ts for use on the Südharzeisenbahn in 1925.

When the Gera to Wuitz-Mumsdorf line closed in 1969, literally worn out and with its dependent lignite seams exhausted, just three locomotives remained in service. These were the Borsig 0-8-0Ts nos 99 5911 and 99 5912 plus the last surviving O & K decapod no. 99 183, the other two having been despatched to Russia in 1945. Following its many years at Eisfeld, the geared axles had proved too complex to maintain and were removed. Consequently, during its final years of service at Gera, the locomotive ran as a 2-6-2T with equally sized wheels. One of the Esslingen 0-10-0Ts no. 99 191 worked at both Eisfeld and Gera between 1944 and 1969, having been transferred to Thüringen from Baden. Although none of the O & K variants of these fascinating 0-10-0Ts have survived, one of the later conventional Esslingen versions has been preserved. Supplied in 1927 to the Nagold-Altensteig line in Baden, no. 99 193 now resides in Switzerland at the CFT Blonay-Chamby.

5.1.   Orenstein & Koppel no. 99 183 was recorded at Gera Pforten in August 1967. Originally built as a 0-10-0T with the outer wheels connected by internal gears on the Luttermöller principal, it was converted to a 2-6-2T with equally sized wheels in 1956 after the gears were removed. During its service on the Gera to Wuitz-Mumsdorf line, it was known as "Fiery Isabella" due to its excessive fuel consumption. (T. Martin).

5.2.   Borsig 0-8-0T no. 99 5911 arrives at Gera Pforten with a short passenger train in August 1967. The formation of two four wheeled coaches and one bogie vehicle was part of a total stock of seven passenger coaches at that time, the line being predominately a freight operation. (T. Martin).

5.3.   Sister locomotive no. 99 5912 being refuelled at Gera depot on the same occasion. The two Borsig 0-8-0Ts were delivered to the line in 1922 and their entire working lives were spent working between Gera and Wuitz-Mumsdorf. (T. Martin).

5.4.   No. 99 5714, the last of the Borsig 0-4-4-0T Mallets supplied to the Gera–Wuitz Mumsdorf line. It was recorded at Gera Pforten in August 1967 shortly after being withdrawn from service. Note the rectangular wooden buffers and the air brake cylinder on top of the side tank – originally two of these had been fitted to the cab roof. (T. Martin).

5.5.   A passenger journey on the route to Wuitz-Mumsdorf was a slow affair, the mixed train shunting stock at many intermediate stations. Borsig 0-4-4-0T Mallet no. 99 5712 runs through the loop at Kayna, the mid point station on the line. The additional high level buffers were for use with standard gauge stock. This scene was recorded on 7th August 1963. (D. Trevor Rowe).

PART TWO
NARROW GAUGE IN THE BALTIC REGION

The area surrounding the Baltic coast in the north east of Germany, comprising the federal region of Mecklenburg-Vorpommern (Mecklenburg-Western Pomerania), was rich in narrow gauge railways. With gauges ranging from 60cm, 75cm, 90cm and metre, the variety and extent of the systems was impressive by any stretch of the imagination. Sadly the 60cm and metre gauge routes have been consigned to history, whilst only one of the 75cm lines has survived into post reunification Germany. Fortunately the remaining 75cm line and the nearby 90cm route, both very different in character, are still providing a year round intensive service as they have done since the latter years of the 19th century.

6.   Bad Doberan to Kühlungsborn - The "Molli"

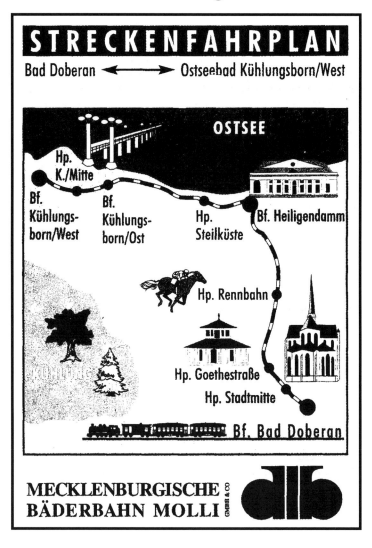

During the 18th century Bad Doberan, near the ancient port of Rostock, had become a favourite resort of the local nobility. These included the Dukes of Mecklenburg and Duke Friedrich Franz 1.

By the later years of the 19th century the main line railway network had reached Rostock, allowing the population as a whole access to this region.

In order to improve the rail access to the coastal towns and villages, a standard gauge branch was opened between Rostock and Bad Doberan in 1883. It was realised that an extension to the coast at the historic fishing village of Heiligendamm, which by that time had been transformed into a popular holiday resort, was essential for the numerous travellers now visiting the area.

For reasons of economy and construction, narrow gauge was deemed necessary for this extension. As a result, a 6.5km line built to the unusual gauge of 90cm was opened in 1886 and was an instant success. The railway and Heiligendamm became very prosperous and neighbouring villages along the coast demanded to be connected in order that they too could reap the benefits. However it would be a further 24 years before this was accomplished, when the 9.6km extension to Ardensee was completed in 1910. By the late 1930s, Ardensee and its adjoining village at Brunshaupten had grown to such an extent that the two merged into a town with a new name of Kühlungsborn in 1938. A total of three stations now serve this sprawling coastal resort, Kühlungsborn Ost, Kühlungsborn Mitte and the terminus at Kühlungsborn West.

Affectionately known as the "Molli", the line was originally a privately owned concern until being absorbed by Deutsche Reichsbahn-Gesellschaft (DRG) in 1920. There have been various suggestions regarding the origin of the name "Molli" that was bestowed upon the railway from its opening date. The most popular of these is that when the first train departed from Bad Doberan, the vast majority of the population witnessed the event. These included a woman with a dog called Molli, who chased the train with its owner running after it calling out the name of the dog. Whether there is any truth in this story is now shrouded in history, but it is a reasonable enough explanation!

In 1945 the DRG became simply Deutsche Reichsbahn (DR) and continued to operate the line until reunification in 1990. With the amalgamation of DR and DB into Deutsche Bahn in 1992, the "Molli" was transferred to yet another owner. This however only lasted until 1995 when the line was privatised. The new company, with substantial backing from the local authorities, is officially called Mecklenburgische Bäderbahn Molli GmbH & Co.KG but is normally known simply as the "Molli".

Although mainly a passenger carrying railway, a limited freight service was operated until 1969. This proved uneconomic due to the change of gauge requiring transhipment, with the increase in road transport it was easier to load the freight directly onto lorries from the standard gauge wagons at either Bad Doberan or Rostock. However the passenger service has always been well patronised and having survived both major conflicts of the 20th Century unharmed, continued to prosper during the austere period of the GDR. There had been two proposals to convert the line to standard gauge, in 1900 and 1924, but in both cases it was deemed too expensive and impractical.

For most travellers on the "Molli", the journey begins at Bad Doberan where the 90cm line shares an island platform with the standard gauge route between Rostock and Wismar. Upon departing from Bad Doberan the train, comprising of up to eight coaches and a parcels van, descends through a pleasant park followed by a level crossing at a busy road junction. Almost immediately the line enters the part of the route for which the "Molli" is renowned throughout the world. This is the section of street running through the centre of the town where the locomotives and rolling stock squeeze their way between the houses and shops along the Molli Strasse, completely ignoring the no entry signs which are erected to warn motor vehicles that it is a one-way street! With its warning bell ringing incessantly to warn motorists and pedestrians alike, all of whom regard the monster in their midst as a normal hourly occurrence, stops are made at halts along the route which are nothing more than bus stops with the passengers lining up on the pavement. During a recent improvement scheme to the town centre, the narrow section of the Molli Strasse has become a pedestrian only area, road vehicles being limited to those delivering goods to the business premises either before 9.30am or after 5.00pm. Despite these recent developments, the remainder of the street running section through the town remains unchanged.

Upon leaving the town, the line runs through a beautiful avenue of lime trees before heading into open countryside leading to Heiligendamm, the major passing place along the route. After the slow cautious journey through the streets of Bad Doberan, a complete change of pace is encountered as the locomotive accelerates to speeds of up to 50 kph. After leaving Heiligendamm the route follows the coast, although the Baltic Sea is not always in view. Three intermediate stations are passed including another short section of street running at Kühlungsborn Mitte before the terminus at Kühlungsborn West is reached, surrounded by impressive villas built in the 19th century. Here are also situated the workshops and depot of the railway, whilst adjacent to the station is a small museum devoted to the history of the line.

The first locomotives used on the initial section of the line were four 0-4-0TR steam powered trams, with fully enclosed motion, built by Krauss of Munich. These were all withdrawn before 1915, by which time the full length of the route to Ardensee had been opened. The extended route required more powerful locomotives in the form of three conventional 0-6-0Ts from Henschel, nos 99 301 to 303, supplied between 1910 and 1914. These were followed by three 0-8-0Ts from the same manufacturer in 1923 and 1924, nos 99 311 to 313. The 0-6-0Ts were withdrawn in 1945 whilst the 0-8-0Ts survived until 1961. At various times during the inter-war period, most of the Henschel locomotives also worked on another 90cm line known as the Rübenbahn that operated near Wismar. This line closed in 1945, which coincided with the withdrawal of the 0-6-0Ts.

In 1932 Orenstein & Koppel produced the three locomotives which have become synonymous with the "Molli". These are the 2-8-2Ts, nos 99 2321-0, 99 2322-8 and 99 2323-6, which are still in regular service today. Their original DRG numbers were 99 321 to 323. These superb superheated machines, which weigh 44 tonnes in working order, develop 460hp and are capable of speeds up to 50 kph. With their angled cab sides, long boilers and side tanks, they have a definite rakish appearance and appear to be completely out of character when making their slow progress through the streets of Bad Doberan.

By 1961 the Henschel 0-8-0Ts had become life expired and were replaced by three second hand locomotives of the same wheel arrangement. These were built by VEB Lokomotivbau "Karl Marx" (LKM) at Bablesberg in 1951 and were closely based on the earlier Henschel design. Originally numbered 99-331 to 333, the first two were superheated whilst 99 333 was saturated. Now renumbered 99 2331-9 and 99 2332-7, the two superheated examples remain at Kühlungsborn whilst no.99 333 was withdrawn in 1969. With a weight of 32 tonnes in working order and a power rating of 320hp, these two relatively modern machines are retained as reserve motive power for their three older companions. Originally acquired for use on freight trains, they are equally at ease hauling passenger trains when deputising for one of the 2-8-2Ts.

Although some of the earlier wooden bodied rolling stock has been retained for traditionszüg trains, the majority of the carriages used currently are modern short bogie coaches of steel construction with the end balconies so characteristic of European minor railways. The livery has, since the opening of the railway, been a colourful red and ivory colour scheme, very similar to that adopted more recently by the Harz network. This attractive livery was retained by DR during their period of operation and has been continued by Mecklenburgische Bäderbahn Molli, who have continued to operate this splendid unique railway very successfully since 1995.

6.1.   Orenstein & Koppel 2-8-2T no. 99 321 was viewed shortly after departing from Bad Doberan station with a train on the "Molli" bound for Kühlungsborn. After crossing the square in the foreground, the route enters the street section for which the "Molli" is highly renowned. This scene was recorded on 22nd May 1966. (D.Trevor Rowe).

6.2.　　From the same location as the above scene, but viewed in the opposite direction. Another of the trio of 2-8-2Ts, no. 099 902-9 (99 322) leaves the Molli-Strasse whilst approaching the station at Bad Doberan on 31st July 1992. (B. Benn).

6.3.　　No. 99 321 hauls a mixed train through the almost deserted main street at Bad Doberan on 22nd May 1966. Note how the street narrows after the road junction the locomotive is just about to cross. (D.Trevor Rowe).

6.4.   On the same occasion, 2-8-2T no. 99 322 was recorded hauling another mixed train from Kühlungsborn through Bad Doberan. As can be seen from the clock, the time was 5.40 pm which probably explains the lack of traffic and pedestrians. (D.Trevor Rowe).

6.5.   A more typical Bad Doberan scene as the same locomotive, now DB no.099 902-9, threads its way among the traffic a few yards further along the street than the last view. Recorded on 30th July 1992, there is certainly an impression of improved prosperity following reunification. (B. Benn).

6.6.   Another view of the Molli-Strasse as no. 99 2322-8 (originally 99 322) heads a train towards Kühlungsborn on 12th May 2004. During recent renovation work, the street has been re-laid in traditional form with new cobbles and flowerbeds constructed in conjunction with a partial pedestrian scheme. This has been implemented only for the relatively short narrow section, the remainder of the street running section remaining unchanged. (J.F.Organ).

6.7.   2-8-2T no. 99 2323-6 passes sister locomotive no. 99 2322-8 at Heiligendamm, the principal passing point on the route. This was the original terminus of the line, before being extended along the coast in 1910. This scene was recorded on 12th May 2004. (J.F.Organ).

6.8.   O & K 2-8-2T no. 099 903-7 (99 323) replenishes its water tanks at Kühlungsborn West, prior to hauling the coaches in the background to Bad Doberan, in June 1995. These rakish locomotives haul their trains at speeds of up to 50 kph along the "country" section of the route, before threading their way slowly through Bad Doberan. (R.White - J.F.Organ. coll).

6.9.   Another view of no.99 2323-6 as it prepares to depart from Kühlungsborn with a typical eight coach "Molli" train to Bad Doberan on 6th April 1999. Note that the leading vehicle is a luggage van. (K. Taylorson).

6.10. LKM built 0-8-0T no. 99 331 was recorded outside the locomotive depot at Kühlungsborn West on 22nd May 1966. Three of these locomotives were supplied second hand in 1961, principally for freight traffic. The two surviving examples have been retained as spare engines and occasionally haul passenger trains if one of the 2-8-2Ts is unavailable, although only 99 331 (99 2331-9) was in service in 2004. (D.Trevor Rowe).

6.11. The other 0-8-0T, no. 99 332, was on static display alongside the small museum at Kühlungsborn West. It would require boiler repairs before returning to service. The 1951 built machine was recorded attached to a preserved parcels van on 12th May 2004. (J.F.Organ).

6.12. A contrast in locomotive design is seen as no. 99 2323-6 departs from Kühlungsborn with no. 99 332 alongside. The handsome lines of the O & K 2-8-2T dating from 1932 compare favourably with the utilitarian appearance of the much younger LKM 0-8-0T. (J.F.Organ).

7. The Island of Rügen

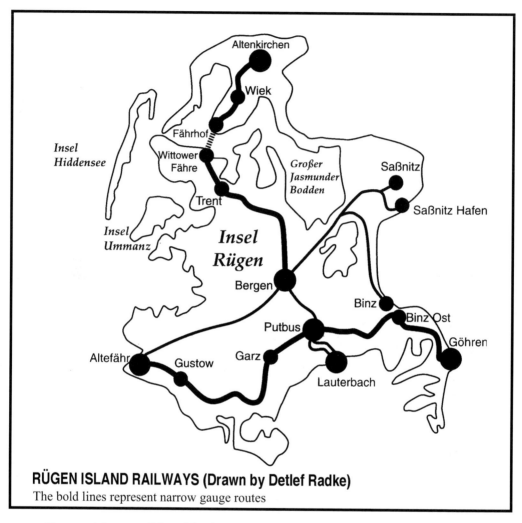

RÜGEN ISLAND RAILWAYS (Drawn by Detlef Radke)
The bold lines represent narrow gauge routes

Germany's largest offshore island, Rügen lies in the Baltic Sea close to the mainland east of Stralsund, from where it is connected by a combined road and rail causeway. In much the same way as the area around Bad Doberan developed as a fashionable resort during the 19th century, Rügen also became a favourite retreat at around the same period.

During the last decade of the 19th century, a 75cm railway was planned to connect the developing resorts in the east of the island with the standard gauge connection further west.

The first section to be completed in 1895 was a 12km line linking Putbus, the major town in the south of the island, with the large resort of Binz on the islands east coast. The following year a 35km route from Putbus to Altefähr in the west was opened which provided the island with a connection to the standard gauge network. Originally the standard gauge line on the island was connected to the mainland by a train ferry. This was replaced in 1936 when the causeway linking Stralsund and Altefähr was constructed. In 1899 the original route to Binz was extended by a further 13km to Göhren, where another popular resort was being developed in the south east of the island.

Meanwhile, an isolated 38km line had been constructed in the north of the island, which linked Bergen with Altenkirchen near the north coast. Opened in 1896, this section included a ferry across a large inlet between Wittower Fähre and Fährhof. Although the ferry carried freight wagons, passengers were obliged to cross as pedestrians and board a waiting train on the other side of the inlet. Consequently, three locomotives and a small rake of coaches were permanently stabled at Altenkirchen to work the 15km section to the north of the ferry crossing.

Originally built and operated by a private company, Rügensche Kleinbahn (Rügen Light Railway), the 98km system survived as an independent concern until 1949, being absorbed by Deutsche Reichsbahn following the creation of the GDR. Known affectionately as Der Rasende Roland (Racing Roland), the railway continued to provide a healthy return of traffic figures for both passenger and freight services until the 1960s. Following World War 2 and the resulting division of Germany, the stretch of coast on the Baltic seaboard between Lübeck and the Polish border became the only area of coastline available to the citizens of East Germany. With a result, the resorts on the south and east of Rügen became a popular destination with a journey along the 75cm gauge railway as an added bonus.

With a gradual improvement in the state of the roads during the 1960s, plus an increase in the use of road transport for freight haulage, the narrow gauge lines in the west and north of the island began to show a decline in patronage. In addition to the increased use of road transport, the standard gauge line that ran diagonally across Rügen linking Altefähr, Bergen and Sassnitz, plus branches to Putbus and Binz, handled the majority of the freight traffic without the need for transhipment. By 1970, only the 25km between Putbus and Göhren remained of the narrow gauge network on the island, this having always boasted the heaviest passenger services. The remaining freight services were withdrawn, leaving this surviving section of the once extensive system as a purely passenger only line. However the following two decades produced an increase in revenue which was complimented by additional investment by DR into the line. As mentioned in the Introduction, the East German Government declared the surviving portion of the system a National Technical Monument in 1975, which secured the future survival of this fascinating railway.

Following reunification, the future of the railway was once again in question. With the amalgamation of DR and DB in 1992, the new regime was just as keen to dispose of this "narrow gauge backwater" as it was with its other minor lines elsewhere. However, local feeling was particularly strong plus the aforementioned Technical Monument status, with the result that the railway and equipment was sold to a private concern in 1996. The new owner was the Karsdofer Eisenbahngesellshaft (KEG) who revived the original name of Rügensche Kleinbahn GmbH & Co. for identification and operating purposes. An intensive year round steam hauled service is provided, although reduced during the winter period, whilst much investment has seen a noticeable improvement in the overhaul appearance of the railway. Consequently the locomotives and rolling stock are immaculately presented whilst the infrastructure has been continually improved since 1996. Despite the use of some modern locomotives, speeds are of necessity low. This is due to the fact that the sub soil of the island is mainly sand and the track is laid onto the soft earth with light ballast. However, the journey through the delightful countryside of Rügen is a fascinating experience, being a veritable time warp from the 19th century. The line was extended in 1999 when the 2km standard gauge branch between Putbus and the coast at Lauterbach was converted to dual gauge. As there is no loop at Lauterbach, the shuttle service on this short section is worked on a "top and tail" system with a diesel locomotive attached to the rear of the train. Early in 2004 the ownership of the railway was transferred from KEG to Eisenbahn-Betriebs-Gesellschaft (EBG) who immediately began to implement a number of improvements to the infrastructure. During the author's visit to Rügen in May 2004, the line was closed temporarily whilst some much needed track repairs were being carried out.

The first locomotives to operate on the Rügen 75cm system were three 0-4-0Ts built by Vulcan at Stettin for the opening of the line in 1895. These were joined by more powerful machines in the form of two 0-4-4-0T Mallets from the same manufacturer in 1902. Three more locomotives, built to the same design by Hanomag, were supplied between 1908 and 1911. However, the locomotives most closely associated with the system arrived in 1913 when Vulcan produced the first of the celebrated 0-8-0WTs. Ultimately three of these superb superheated machines were supplied, the others arriving in 1914 and 1925. Originally numbered 51, 52 and 53, they ultimately became DR nos 99 4631-99 4633. These were the principal locomotives on the island for many years, aided by the Mallets and some Hartmann 0-4-4-0T Saxon-Meyers that were transferred there in the 1920s for use mainly on the Bergen to Wittower Fähre route and the isolated section to Altenkirchen. Ultimately a total of nine Meyers worked in the island, although not all at the same time. Following their arrival from Saxony, the Meyers were fitted with air braking systems in order to be compatible with the rolling stock. This resulted in the air cylinders being placed on top of the boiler which somewhat detracted from the handsome appearance of these attractive locomotives.

By 1965, many of the older locomotives had been withdrawn, being replaced by newer machines inherited from closed lines elsewhere in the GDR. Two Henschel 2-8-0Ts dating from 1938 were transferred from the recently closed Kleinbahn Kreis Jerichow 1, west of Berlin. These powerful superheated locomotives, nos 99 4801 and 99 4802, were a much appreciated addition to the stock, working alongside the three Vulcan 0-8-0WTs. For the isolated section north of the ferry between Fährof and Altenkirchen two former Heeresfeldbahn locomotives, which had previously worked on the Jüterbog-Luckenwalder Kreiskleinbahn south of Berlin, were also transferred to Rügen in 1965. These were 0-6-0TTs built by Henschel in 1941, similar to a large number of locomotives built by Jung

and BMF for the German army. Some of these worked in Austria following World War 2 whilst one of the Jung examples now works in France at Abreschviller, having been converted to 70cm gauge. (see *Northern France Narrow Gauge* and *Austrian Narrow Gauge*, for more details of these exiled locomotives). The two Henschel machines based at Altenkirchen were numbered 99 4651 and 99 4652. Another locomotive that was based at Altenkirchen during the 1960s was the much travelled 0-6-0T no. 99 4511. Originally built by Krauss as a 0-6-2T in 1899, this was completely rebuilt at Görlitz in 1965 and now resides at the Pressnitztalbahn in Saxony.

The most dramatic arrivals on the island occurred in 1983 and 1984 when two of the LKM class V11K neu 2-10-2Ts were transferred from Saxony. Numbered 99 782 and 99 784, these powerful locomotives appeared initially to be too large and overweight for the lightly laid track. However they have proved to be a sound investment, being joined by no. 99 783 a decade later. They continue to handle the majority of the traffic on the line being maintained in immaculate condition, as are the other surviving locomotives on the island.

The current locomotive fleet consists of the two remaining Vulcan 0-8-0WTs, nos 52 and 53, both having been superbly restored to their original green livery and numbers at Görlitz in 1992. These are the only surviving machines originally supplied for service on Rügen. The remaining active machines consist of the two Henschel 2-8-0Ts and three LKM 2-10-2Ts, all seven locomotives being regularly seen in service although the 2-10-2Ts are the normal motive power. In addition, one of the Henschel 0-6-0TTs, no. 99 4652 is on static display at Putbus together with a rake of historic rolling stock. The other Vulcan 0-8-0WT no.51 (99 4631) is due to return to the line in the near future, following many years in a private collection.

Two diesel locomotives are also based at Putbus. A former Heeresfeldbahn type HF-130C 0-6-0, which was constructed by Gmeinder in 1944, performs the station shunting duties. Formerly no. 100.902, it arrived on Rügen in 1964 and was renumbered Köf 6003 after privatisation in 1996. Another Gmeinder built machine is no. V 51 901, a powerful Bo-Bo central cab locomotive dating from 1964, which originally worked in West Germany near Stuttgart. It arrived at Putbus in 1999 and is used as a relief locomotive and for hauling the shuttle services along the dual gauge branch to Lauterbach.

Also stationed at Putbus are two privately owned locomotives that make occasional appearances hauling special trains. These are the other Henschel 0-6-0TT, originally 99 4651, and another former Heeresfeldbahn locomotive in the shape of the 1939 built Borsig 0-10-0TT that worked in Austria between 1945 and 1983. This operated on the Salzkammergut-Lokalbahn, where it was their number 22 until 1957, when it was transferred to the Zillertalbahn and became no.4. Finally it was transferred to the Bregenzerwaldbahn in 1974 until it returned to its homeland in 1983. Both these locomotives are immaculately preserved in an attractive blue livery and have received names. The Henschel is named *Nicki+Frank S* after the children of the owner, whilst the Borsig is now known as *Aquarius C*. The latter was named *Castle Caereinion* during the period it was based at Jenbach, in recognition of the Zillertalbahn's close links with the Welshpool and Llanfair Railway.

The rolling stock comprises of a variety of end balcony coaches, some of which date from the earlier period of the railways operation. The majority of the current service trains utilise more recent vehicles dating from the 1960s. Although freight traffic is no longer carried on the line, a large number of wagons and vans survive. Many of these are used on traditionszüg demonstration freight or mixed trains, which operate occasionally throughout the summer. The service trains invariably include a vehicle that has been converted into a bicycle van. With cycling one of the major pastimes on Rügen, this service is in constant demand. The vans, at least one of which is a new vehicle specifically designed for the purpose, can carry up to 20 bicycles.

7.1.   On the Island of Rügen, Vulcan 0-8-0WT no. 99 4632 was recorded departing from Altefähr with a heavy mixed train on 24th May 1966. This section of the 75cm gauge line on the island closed in 1967, connection with the standard gauge network now being confined to Putbus. (D.Trevor Rowe).

7.2.   This is one of the Hartmann built Meyers that were transferred to Rügen from Saxony during the 1920s. No. 99 553 is seen at Puddemin on the line to Altefähr with a freight train on 24th May 1966. Note the overgrown and obviously little used track in the foreground. (D.Trevor Rowe).

7.3.   Putbus is now the western terminus of the Rügen narrow gauge line, in addition to being the operating "hub" of the system. LKM built 2-10-2T no. 99 782 basks in the evening sun at the platform while awaiting departure to Göhren on 7th April 1999. Judging by the displaced set of points in the foreground, some track replacement work was in progress at that time. (K.Taylorson).

7.4.   This Gmeinder Bo-Bo diesel locomotive, built in 1964, arrived on the island from Stuttgart in 1999. It is currently used for "top and tailing" the shuttle trains along the short dual gauge branch to Lauterbach Mole, in addition to other duties such as relief engine, and was viewed at Putbus on 13th May 2004. (J.F.Organ).

7.5.   At the principal intermediate station of Binz Ost, 0-8-0WT no. 99 4632-8 prepares to depart with a passenger train bound for Putbus on 14th September 1981. Prior to the arrival of the three LKM 2-10-2Ts, the Vulcan 0-8-0WTs handled the majority of the traffic on the southern section of the island's 75cm system. (K.Taylorson).

7.6.   Two of the LKM 2-10-2Ts pass at Binz Ost. No. 99 784 awaits departure with a Putbus to Göhren train whilst no. 99 782 arrives with a train from Göhren on 7th April 1999. (K.Taylorson).

7.7.   One of the two Henschel 2-8-0Ts transferred to Rügen from Brandenburg in 1965. Shortly after its arrival on the island, no. 99 4802 prepares to depart from Binz Ost on 24th May 1966 with a train bound for Göhren. (D.Trevor Rowe).

7.8.   The first of the Vulcan 0-8-0WTs, no. 99 4631 built in 1913, was recorded at Sellin between Göhren and Binz whilst hauling a heavy mixed train on 24th May 1966. (D.Trevor Rowe).

7.9.   Beautifully restored to its original green livery and number, the last of the Vulcan 0-8-0WTs, no.53 dating from 1925, waits at the eastern terminus at Göhren prior to hauling a train to Putbus in June 1995. (R.White -J.F.Organ. coll).

7.10.   0-8-0WT no.99 4631 prepares to depart from Göhren with a mixed train for Putbus on 2th May 1966. The scene looks almost Mediterranean rather than the far north of Europe on the Baltic Coast. (D.Trevor Rowe).

7.11.   The majority of the services are now handled by the three LKM 2-10-2Ts transferred from Saxony during the 1980s and 90s. No. 99 784 was recorded running around its train at Göhren before returning to Putbus on 7th April 1999. (K.Taylorson).

7.12.   On the northern section of the Rügen system, now sadly closed, a number of the 0-4-4-0T Meyers transferred from Saxony were the usual motive power for many years. No. 99 552 was viewed arriving at the intermediate station, bearing the very English name of *Trent* on 25th May 1966. (D.Trevor Rowe).

7.13.   Meyer no. 99 570 alongside the Baltic Sea at Wittower Fähre on the same occasion. Note that these locomotives were fitted with air braking after their transfer to the island, hence the array of air cylinders mounted on top of the boiler. (D.Trevor Rowe).

7.14.   Having completed its shunting manoeuvres, no. 99 570 prepares to depart from Wittower Fähre with a train bound for Bergen. Note the grass-strewn track and sandy sub soil, so typical of the island. (D. Trevor Rowe).

7.15.   Earlier the same day, Meyer no. 99 570 was shunting wagons onto the ferry at Wittower Fähre, the wheelhouse of which can be seen behind the locomotive. The unique narrow gauge train ferry conveyed freight stock to the isolated section of line, situated on the far side of the large inlet in the north of the island. (D. Trevor Rowe).

7.16. On the other side of the ferry crossing, Henschel 0-6-0TT no. 99 4651 was shunting the wagons of a mixed train onto the ferry at Fährhof on 25th May 1966. The coaches remained on "terra firma" whilst the occupants crossed as foot passengers. (D. Trevor Rowe).

7.17. Some remedial work is being attended to the track at Wiek, on the isolated section in the north of the island, whilst no. 99 4651 passes some precariously loaded hay wagons en route to Fährhof on the same occasion. (D. Trevor Rowe).

7.18.   No. 99 4651 simmers outside the small shed at Altenkirchen which was, at that time, the most northerly station in the GDR. Alongside the shed is the 0-6-0T no. 99 4511 which had recently been transferred to Rügen. (D.Trevor Rowe).

7.19.   A more detailed view of no. 99 4511 at Altenkirchen. Originally constructed by Krauss in 1899 as a 0-6-2T for the Rathenow-Senzke-Nauen line in Brandenburg, this locomotive led a nomadic existence until it was rebuilt as a 0-6-0T at Görlitz in 1965. It is now preserved at the Pressnitztalbahn in Saxony. (D.Trevor Rowe)

8. Metre Gauge routes in the Baltic area

On the Baltic mainland, an extensive metre gauge network with its headquarters at Stralsund operated between 1895 and 1969. Known as the Franzburger Kreisbahnen, the 66km system was a typical rural railway that provided a useful passenger and freight service throughout the area. The main route of the system linked Stralsund to Damgarten via Barth whilst a branch line linked Altenpleen and Klausdorf. The heaviest traffic was on the route between Stralsund and Barth, a fishing port 30km to the west, which was the last section to remain in operation.

A variety of locomotives worked on the system during its existence of 76 years, aided by some Wismar twin vehicle railcar sets during the final period of operation. Initially six, relatively small, 0-4-0WTs were supplied by the local manufacturer, Vulcan at Stettin. This town, one of the largest in the area, was ceded to Poland following World War 2 and its name changed to Szczecin. In 1902, two larger locomotives were supplied to assist these lightweight machines. The new arrivals were both 0-4-4-0T Mallets, also built by Vulcan, which remained in service on the line until its closure in 1969. Their DR numbers were 99 5621 and 99 5622.

In 1928 a second hand Henschel 0-6-0T, no.99 5611 built in 1903, was acquired to assist the Mallets and the remaining examples of the 0-4-0WTs. The Henschel worked until the line closed and still survives. In 1972 it was sold to Les Chemins de Fer Régioneaux (CFR) in France, together with no.99 5001, a Borsig 0-4-0T that had previously been employed on shunting duties at Wernigerode Westerntor Works on the Harz network. The CFR operated the northern section of the Vivarais system between 1970 and 1987, the two German locomotives being imported due to the unavailability of suitable French motive power. After the demise of the CFR, the two locomotives were placed in store at the home of their owner at Valence, where presumably they still reside.

One of the line's original Vulcan 0-4-0WTs has also survived into preservation. It now works on the Kleinbahn-Museumbahn at Bruchhausen-Vilsen to the south of Bremen.

8.1. Situated on the mainland close to Rügen was the metre gauge Franzburger Kreisbahnen system. Vulcan 0-4-4-0T Mallet no. 99 5622 prepares to depart from Altenpleen with a passenger train on 23rd May 1966. (D.Trevor Rowe).

8.2.   No. 99 5622 pauses outside the shed at Barth, which is a busy fishing port on the Baltic coast. The branch from Stralsund to Barth was the last section of this once extensive system to remain in operation, until it was closed in 1970. (D.Trevor Rowe).

8.3.   The Franzburger Kreisbahnen relied on railcars for the majority of its passenger services during the later days of its existence. A Wismar two car set was viewed departing from Stralsund en route to Barth on 23rd May 1966. (D.Trevor Rowe).

9. 60cm Rails in Mecklenburg-Western Pomerania

The 60cm system in the area was the Mecklenburg-Pommersche Schmalspurbahn (MPSB), an extensive network that radiated from Friedland. In its heyday during the 1930s, the network totalled 216km with 44 locomotives on the stock list. Opened in 1892, part of the system survived until 1970 when economics forced the closure of the final 50km section. The principal stations on the system included Anklam, Uhlenhorst and Wegezin-Dennin, all situated in the north east corner of Germany near the present day border with Poland. Operating both freight and passenger services through this sparsely inhabited, mainly rural area, it was incredible that it survived as long as it did. In many ways it resembled the sugar beet lines of Northern France, carrying mainly agricultural merchandise across a similar landscape.

The motive power was provided by a diverse collection of machinery. These ranged from some diminutive 0-4-0TTs built by Henschel and Krauss-Maffei, 0-6-2WTTs from Jung and some large 0-8-0 tender locomotives produced by both Vulcan and Orenstein & Koppel. Interestingly, three of the surviving engines came to the UK after the MPSB closed in 1970, although only one now remains here. This is a Jung 0-6-2WTT dating from 1908, no. 99 3353, that was acquired by the fledgling Brecon Mountain Railway. Following a comprehensive overhaul at Pant, the German locomotive has been in regular service at the Brecon line since it opened in 1981. Another locomotive of the same class, no.99 3351 of 1906, was sold to the USA in 1970. This returned to Germany in 1999 and is now on display in the Feldbahn Museum at Frankfurt am Main. These useful machines could be used with or without their tenders, consequently they would often be seen working as 0-6-2WTs.

The other locomotives imported to the UK in 1971 were two of the large superheated 0-8-0s, which were acquired by a company set up to purchase the Vale of Rheidol line from British Railways. These comprised of a Vulcan built in 1925 (no. 99 3461) and an Orenstein & Koppel dating from 1934 (no. 99 3462). The Vulcan spent a short time working at Knebworth Park in Hertfordshire before being placed in store at New Romney. The O&K locomotive was initially sent to Carnforth for a short period, following which it was transferred to the Boston Lodge works at the Ffestiniog Railway for some boiler repairs. Following the failure of the company to secure the ownership of the Rheidol line, the two locomotives were sold in 1978. Ironically, the Rheidol line was to be sold a decade later to the company that operates the Brecon Mountain line. Following their sale, the two powerful 0-8-0s returned to mainland Europe. No. 99 3461 now works on the Froissy- Cappy- Dompierre line in the north of France whilst 99 3462 returned to Germany where it now forms part of a private collection near Bielefeld.

9.1.   The extensive 60cm Mecklenburg-Pommersche Schmalspurbahnen at one time boasted a colossal route mileage of 216km and a fleet of 44 locomotives. By the 1960s, the majority had closed leaving only the 50km route between Anklam and Friedland as the last surviving section. Jung 0-6-2WTT no. 99 3351 pauses at Wegezin with a passenger train on a dull 26th May 1966. This locomotive now resides in the Feldbahn Museum at Frankfurt whilst sister no. 99 3353 is based in the UK at the Brecon Mountain Railway. (D.Trevor Rowe).

9.2.   On the same occasion, no. 99 3351 receives attention at the junction station of Wegezin-Dennin. Following the closure of the MPSB in 1970, this 1906 built locomotive spent many years in the USA before being repatriated in 1998. (D.Trevor Rowe).

9.3.   Vulcan 0-8-0 no. 99 3461 shunting wagons at Wegezin-Dennin during the course of hauling a mixed train from Anklam to Freidland on 26th May 1966. (D.Trevor Rowe).

9.4.   The shunting operation involved occupying a level crossing positioned very close to a set of points. Fortunately road traffic was minimal so very little disruption was caused. (D.Trevor Rowe).

9.5.   Having completed shunting the stock, no. 99 3461 sets off from Wegezin-Dennin towards Freidland. After the MPSB closed, this locomotive spent a number of years stored in the UK with the intention of it working on the Vale of Rheidol line. Following the failure of that scheme, it was transferred to its current home, the CFT Froissy-Cappy-Dompierre in Northern France. (D.Trevor Rowe).

9.6.   The Vulcan 0-8-0 arrives at Freidland with its mixed train. The freight haulage was mainly agricultural, sugar beet being one of the principal sources of revenue. This view from May 1966 shows the extensive track layout at the southern terminus. (D. Trevor Rowe).

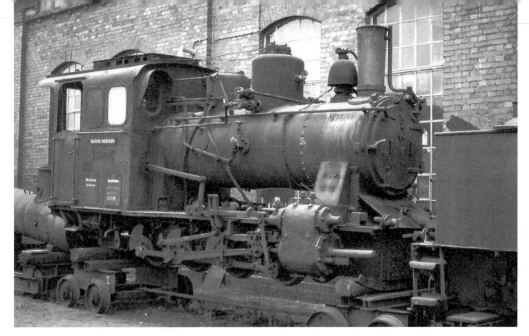

9.7. The Orenstein & Koppel 0-8-0, no. 99 3462 was recorded at Görlitz works in 1967 after withdrawal from service due to boiler problems. This was shortly prior to its purchase and transfer to Great Britain for the proposed Vale of Rheidol scheme. (J.B.Snell).

10. The 75cm Systems in Brandenburg

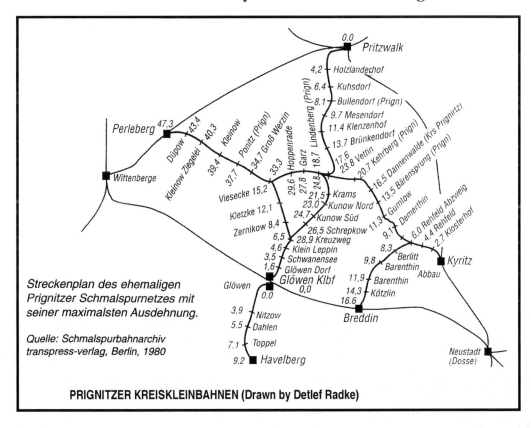

PRIGNITZER KREISKLEINBAHNEN (Drawn by Detlef Radke)

To the south of Mecklenburg is the state of Brandenburg, within which Berlin is a separate enclave. The area once boasted numerous 75cm lines dating from the final decade of the 19th Century. These included the Prignitzer Kreiskleinbahnen situated to the north west of Berlin, the Kleinbahn Kreis Jerichow1 and Rathenow-Senzke-Nauen, both of which were to the west of the capital, and the Jüterbog-Luckenwalder Kreiskleinbahnen to the south. All apart from the first named were closed by 1965, the surviving line remaining in operation until 1974.

Motive power on all the lines comprised largely of 0-6-0Ts from various manufacturers including Orenstein & Koppel, Hartmann and Krauss. The major exception was the Jerichow line, which in 1912 and 1922 took delivery of five splendid 0-8-0Ts from O & K, nos 99 4551 and 99 4641- 4645. These were joined in 1938 by two Henschel 2-8-0Ts nos 99 4801 and 99 4802 which, as noted previously, are now based at Rügen. These powerful superheated 2-8-0Ts were similar to the 90cm 2-8-2Ts supplied by O&K to the "Molli" in 1932. After World War 2 the Jüterbog line inherited two Henschel designed 0-6-0TT locomotives, built in 1941 for the Heeresfeldbahnen (German Army), nos 99 4651and 4652 plus another machine of the same type built by Jung in 1944, no. 99 4653. These provided the mainstay of motive power for the line until it closed in 1965. Like the larger Henschel 2-8-0Ts at Jerichow, two of these 0-6-0TTs migrated to Rügen in 1965 where the two Henschel examples found useful employment on the isolated section between Fährhof and Altenkirchen.

The most extensive and longest survivor of these lines was the 135km Prignitzer Kreiskleinbahnen, which began operations in 1892. It served a largely rural area, the major centres being Kyritz, Pritzwalk and Havelberg with the small town of Lindenberg roughly in the centre of the system. Like the other lines in the area it relied upon a fleet of modest 0-6-0Ts for its motive power requirements, supplemented by some primitive railcars for lighter passenger duties in later years. During the early 1950s, three of the illustrious 0-4-4-0T Saxon-Meyers, nos 99 557, 99 576 and 99 593, were transferred to Brandenburg from Saxony to assist the smaller locomotives. These were joined in 1965 by four of the Orenstein & Koppel 0-8-0Ts, nos 99 4641-4645, which were transferred from the Jerichow line. During the final decade of the line's existence, these powerful locomotives provided the majority of the motive power requirements for both freight and passenger services. During this final period of the operation, the 0-8-0Ts and Meyers were joined by the Krauss / Görlitz 0-6-0T no. 99 4511 following its tenure at Rügen. Sadly the line closed in 1971 which effectively ended the narrow gauge presence in Brandenburg. Much of the system had in fact closed in 1969, the isolated 9km branch between Glöwen and Havelberg surviving for a further two years.

Following 23 years of closure, steam returned to the area in 1994 thanks to the efforts of a preservation group known as the Prignitzer Kleinbahnmuseum who have reinstated 9km of track between Lindenberg and Mesendorf. Some of the original rolling stock has been rescued and restored, some of the items having spent the intervening years as garden sheds and other domestic purposes. The only survivor of the O & K 0-8-0Ts, no. 99 4644, was removed from the plinth at Neustrelitz it had stood on since 1969 to be restored to working order. Currently this is the only steam locomotive based at Lindenberg, the other items of motive power being three industrial diesels built by LKM. However the museum has close links with the Pressnitztalbahn in Saxony where 99 4511 is currently based. It is quite possible that this well travelled locomotive will return to Lindenberg in the near future, either on a temporary visit or a permanent basis.

10.1.   The Prignitzer Kreiskleinbahnen was the last surviving 75cm gauge line in Brandenburg. Orenstein & Koppel 0-8-0T no. 99 4645 is about to depart from Kyritz with a train bound for Lindenberg and Pritzwalk on 29th May 1966. (D. Trevor Rowe).

10.2.   During the same journey, no.99 4645 pauses before crossing the main street at Gumtow. Despite the lack of gates protecting the level crossing, the amount of road traffic appears to be almost non-existent which rendered any extra protection unnecessary! (D. Trevor Rowe).

10.3.   Another O & K 0-8-0T no. 99 4644 hauls a short mixed train along the branch between Glöwen and Havelberg on 28th May 1966. Both nos 99 4644 and 99 4645 worked on the Kleinbahn Kreis Jerichow 1 until they were transferred to the Prignitzer system in 1965. Following closure of the system in 1971,no. 99 4644 was placed on a plinth at Neustrelitz until 1994, when it was restored by the preservation group based at Lindenberg in 1994. (D.Trevor Rowe).

10.4.   No. 99 4645 was recorded with a short freight train at Viesecke, a junction on the route between Kyritz and Perleberg, on 29th May 1966. (D.Trevor Rowe).

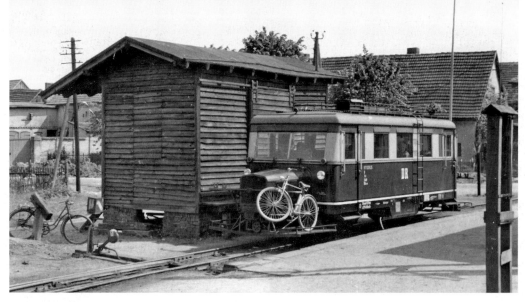

10.5.   Situated roughly in the centre of the Prignitzer Kreiskleinbahnen network was the small town of Lindenberg, which is currently the base for the restored section of line. With a bicycle securely attached to the luggage rack alongside the bonnet, a 1939 built Wismar four-wheeled railcar will soon depart for Kyritz on the same occasion. One assumes the bicycle was owned by a passenger, or was it for the use of the driver in an emergency? (D.Trevor Rowe).

POSTSCRIPT

Following the major political changes in Germany during the last decade, it is almost a miracle that any of the narrow gauge railways described in this publication have survived at all. Thanks to the intervention of dynamic private companies, the continued operation of the majority of lines that survived reunification has been achieved. Obviously the transport requirements of the 21st century are far removed from those even during the later years of the GDR, consequently the new operators are providing services more attuned to the tourist industry rather than daily transport needs. However the fact that the systems have survived is a credit to the enthusiasm of their new owners.

Ffestiniog Travel, Harbour Station, Porthmadog, LL49 9NF (Tel:- 01766 516050) provide a comprehensive continental rail travel service. They can also assist in planning a "tailor made" itinerary to suit any individual requirements. Destinations in Germany are often included in their European holidays, including many of the lines covered in this publication. Indeed, a visit to the Harz network has become an annual event in recent years.Tickets for the independent and museum railways listed below, have to be purchased locally.

Harzer Schmalspurbahnen GmbH (HSB), Friedrichstrasse 151, 38855 Wernigerode, Germany.

Mecklenburgische Bäderbahn Molli GmbH & Co, Am Bahnhof, 18209 Bad Doberan, Germany.

Prignitzer Kleinbahnmuseum, Lindenberg e.V. Hauptstrasse 7, 16928 Lindenberg, Germany.

Rügensche Kleinbahn GmbH & Co, Binzer Strasse 12, 18581 Putbus, Rügen, Germany.

The HSB issue a Rover Ticket allowing unlimited travel for a set period throughout their large system. This is an excellent investment, allowing considerable savings compared to purchasing individual tickets for each journey.

MP Middleton Press

Easebourne Lane, Midhurst
West Sussex. GU29 9AZ

A-0 906520 B-1 873793 C-1 901706 D-1 904474

OOP Out of Print at time of printing - Please check current availability **BROCHURE AVAILABLE SHOWING NEW TITLES**
Tel:01730 813169   www.middletonpress.com   email:info@middletonpress.co.uk